'Jody makes meditation cool, spreading her amazing message of self-love and how to reconnect with your true self, this book is a game changer.'
Madeleine Shaw - Bestselling Author, Health Coach, Yoga Teacher

'Jody is absolutely amazing, I'm incredibly inspired by her energy. She's kept me grounded and allowed me to let go of things that were holding me back.'
Ella Mills - Founder of Deliciously Ella and the MaE Deli

'Jody completely disarmed me. Her bubbly, smiley, easy-going demeanour belie a very deep, powerful and spiritual gift'
Eminé Rushton -Wellness Director, *PSYCHOLOGIES* magazine

'Jody is such a beautiful beam of light. She is a vibrant channel for us to clear out the old and see the truth of what we really are. Grateful to have her as a mentor and get to call her my friend.'
Ashley Roberts - Music Artist, TV Presenter, Model

'Jody has that rare ability to speak directly to the deepest part of you, but rather than simply identifying the blockages that might be getting in your way, she'll also arm you with the advice and practical Tools to work through them, so you can face the world feeling stronger, more connected and more you.'
Joanna McGarry - Beauty Director at large, *Stylist* Magazine

'Jody makes it cool to look within, remove the blocks, love yourself and go get what you desire!'
Jasmine Hemsley - Wellbeing expert, Author and Chef

Jody Shield is a motivational speaker, author, blogger / vlogger, meditation guide and intuitive healer. Her name is reverently whispered among London's high fliers as the go-to healer for all our modern woes. She supports people in processing the past, being present and creating a life they love. She's the first European meditation ambassador for global brand Lululemon Athletica, and has sell-out residencies globally with her own LifeTonic events. Formerly a business director in advertising, Jody has first-hand experience of the stress epidemic that plagues the corporate world. As a consultant, she now works with brands such as Nike, Stella McCartney, Swarovski, Live Nation and Clarins to inspire, teach and change lives. She is a regular speaker at popular events such as *Stylist* Live, Be:Fit, *Marie Claire* Fit Fest and *Red* magazine's Smart Women Week. Jody writes for the *Huffington Post* UK and has been featured in *The Sunday Times*, *Stylist*, *Red*, *PSYCHOLOGIES*, *Women's Health*, *Metro*, *Glamour*, Get the Gloss, Byrdie UK, the Lifestyle Edit, Sheerluxe.com, the Numinous and Hip & Healthy. Jody has launched LifeTonic TV on YouTube.

LifeTonic

A Modern Toolkit to Help You Heal
Your Life and Soothe Your Soul

Jody Shield

yellow
kite

First published in Great Britain in 2017 by Yellow Kite
An imprint of Hodder & Stoughton
An Hachette UK company

1

Trade Paperback ISBN 978 1 473 64060 3
Ebook ISBN 978 1 473 64061 0

Typeset in Sabon MT by Palimpsest Book Production Limited,
Falkirk, Stirlingshire

Printed and bound by Clays Ltd, St Ives plc

Hodder & Stoughton policy is to use papers that are natural,
renewable and recyclable products and made from wood grown in
sustainable forests. The logging and manufacturing processes are
expected to conform to the environmental regulations of
the country of origin.

Yellow Kite
Hodder & Stoughton Ltd
Carmelite House
50 Victoria Embankment
London EC4Y 0DZ

www.yellowkitebooks.co.uk
www.hodder.co.uk

To my spiritual sisters, Lauren and Dalia –
the other two points of my triangle.

Contents

Introduction

Hey, you! You've found this book. Welcome!

Sssshhhh. There's something magical happening right now. You're reading this because you're ready for big transformations and a brighter, richer and more exciting life. You're ready to shake things up. Am I right?

Do you want to:

- Learn how to let go of painful baggage from the past?
- Come to a new understanding of yourself, and gain fresh modern insights about the way the universe works?
- Enrich your life on every level and start to achieve your true potential?
- Learn how to sparkle and shine from the inside out?
- Get high on life?
- Heal your heart and transform your relationships?
  Or all of the above?

That's exactly what this book is for, and I'm excited because I get to go on the journey with you. You, me and these glorious pages of healing are going to be BFFs for the next few weeks, months or years, depending on how you decide to use them.

Perfect timing

I bet this book has dropped into your lap at a time when you most need it. You might not even know you need it yet.

Books have a tendency to appear in your life when you're looking for answers.

There's a wise Zen saying that goes, "When the student is ready, the teacher appears", and it's always spot on. Once you start being aware of this, you'll notice it happening all the time.

I've come to believe that life is an infinite healing journey, packed full of lessons and juicy gifts. Some of us know this already and we're on the path: accelerating, healing, manifesting and experiencing miracles every day. Most people remain unaware and are plodding along, getting more and more frustrated and stuck, or depressed and sad. What would you rather be? Closed and blocked off to the wonder of life, or curious, excited, willing to be open and ready to expand beyond your wildest dreams?

This book is dedicated to all you beautiful people who want to improve your lives. Are you tired of the same cycles? Stuck in a boring job? Over-anxious? Burned out, lost, stressed and disillusioned with your life?

This used to be me, only I didn't know it at the time.

Back in 2009 I was living an ordinary life. Working in a top ad agency in London, helping to manage one of their biggest accounts. Life seemed good. I thought I had it all: perfect job, perfect social life. But behind the scenes, something was awry. I had trouble working out how I genuinely felt about things; it was as if I was blocked and unable to access the deeper layers. It took a lot to make me crack, because I was good at pretending life was brilliant, and I was always "fine" if anyone asked.

A two-week illness caused by stress and anxiety forced me to reevaluate. A few days later, I'd booked a one-way ticket to South America. I wanted answers, a total reboot and a fresh, exciting, new adventure. Which was exactly what I got: a full-on, mind-altering, radical transformation that changed my life for ever.

When I left South America, I was wide-eyed, bushy-tailed and thirsty for knowledge. Six years later and here I am, writing my first book. And that's something I never imagined in my wildest dreams!

Modern spirituality

I'm now a spiritual healer for the modern day, a new leader in the self-help movement, offering a fresh voice to the masses. My light turns on when I'm teaching powerful Tools and techniques that inspire people to take steps to heal. I work with big groups or individuals, and I also speak on stage to hundreds of people at a time. I love sharing my experiences, and new things I've discovered.

If the word "spiritual" makes you tense up a bit, or even think of discarding this book, don't worry. I'm far from the stereotypical spiritual healer – whatever you imagine that to be. I don't wear hemp clothes or long, white robes. You'll find me in leather jackets and faux fur, designer beanies and bright red lipstick. The aged Western concept of the "healer" is one I struggled with when I was coming out of the spiritual closet. At one point, I was worried I might have to join a hippie commune with free sex, harps and lentils, and I nearly turned my back on it all. Thank God that wasn't the case.

As a modern healer, I create my own rules (rules are great if they're your own) and every day I remind myself that there's no set way of doing this. There's no structure to follow, nothing to conform to, and I can do this my way. You can too. Whatever your current views on spirituality, you can take the ideas in this book and make them work in the way that feels most useful and authentic for you.

I'm offering simple, practical, relatable teachings suitable for everyone, no matter what you believe in. And yes, I am spiritual, but that doesn't mean you have to be. It's enough to be you, and willing to be open to hearing what I have to say.

———

You're reading this book for the right reasons, so trust yourself, and know that only positive things will happen.

———

When you invest in yourself and your self-care, there are no negative experiences. What have you got to lose?

There's no one else who can do what you do, your way. You are unique. We all are. This is important to understand. There aren't any completely new ideas in the world – we are all inspired by others – but there are unique expressions of ideas, and your expression will be yours alone.

Radical life changes

If I'd known that I was wasting my time with my marketing degree because I was destined to become a spiritual healer, I'd have felt less guilty missing all those lectures. I'd also have choked on my potato waffles and baked beans. I had zero interest in wellbeing, healing or anything that was remotely good for me. I didn't exercise, I ate frozen, microwave meals and drank copious amounts of snake-bite at the student union. Yet somehow, against all the odds, here I am. It's safe to say, I couldn't have made this up if I'd tried.

My intention for this book is to provide a revolutionary experience for you, designed to transform you at the highest level and shift you up a gear in life. It'll take you on a powerful journey, with an invitation to go inside and explore your inner world. You'll learn to feel your feelings, understand yourself better, and heal from the inside out.

We are all walking history books, crammed full of human "baggage". The baggage contains old memories and emotions from traumatic experiences in our past. There will be many traumas we don't even remember, because we're exceptionally good at hiding them away. Our fear is that one day this baggage will spill out onto the street for all the world to see. That would not be pretty, especially in front of our friends or partners. So we push it down deeper into storage. We pack it in tightly, and hope that one day we'll be brave enough to face it. For some people, the day never comes, and that is a real shame.

The good news is that unpacking the baggage doesn't have to be traumatic. As long as you feel safe and held, you'll have little trauma or reenactment of what you went through initially. And I'm here to hold you.

I'll share with you my own story of the struggles when I was exploring my baggage and learning to let it go, and I hope this will inspire you to believe that no matter what you're facing now, not only is it possible to heal yourself completely, but you will emerge out the other side feeling stronger, braver and more whole than ever.

Tonics and Tools

In the first eight chapters of the book I'll explain some important principles about the mistakes we can all make in life, using my own experiences as illustrations. I'll show you what causes modern ailments such as:

- low self-esteem;
- sadness/depression;
- self-limiting beliefs and self-sabotage;
- procrastination;

- relationship difficulties;
- lack of confidence;
- fear/anxiety.

There's a space to pause and chill out, then from Chapter 10 onwards, the "LifeTonics" will explain how to heal one particular aspect of yourself. They will give you Tools for nourishing your mind, body and soul, and simple techniques that can be easily integrated into your day-to-day life.

Work through the book at your own pace and in the order that seems best, but don't skip any chapters altogether. As I'll explain later, if you feel tempted to skip something, it probably means that's the topic you most need to face.

This is going to be a journey with purpose and soul, a remedy for your hectic life. I hope you will come out the other side ready to change your world.

Enjoy your time with this book, be curious about what you'll find, honour the "gifts" and let's get excited about life again!

With love and light,
Jody xx

PART ONE

Getting Started

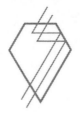

CHAPTER 1

The Making of Me

I was raised in Liverpool in the '80s, where home was a beautiful white Victorian house by the River Mersey. As grand as it looked from the outside, inside it was slowly crumbling away, and there was always work to be done: wallpaper peeling off, chipped paint, funny smells and a leaky roof. It was old but shabby chic, full of vintage objects passed down through the ancestors, and acquired over the years.

My parents were hard-working entrepreneurs who were driven, inspiring and ambitious. Mum won awards for her French bistro, a bustling basement restaurant in the centre of town, and Dad was a lawyer during the day, and a barman at night in the bistro. Somehow they managed to juggle two kids, their busy careers and entertaining clients day and night. Luckily we had nannies, babysitters, neighbours and grannies who took it in turn to look after us. Mum and Dad did the best they could to keep everyone happy, while maintaining their own sanity and keeping the family together.

Blessed with a privileged childhood, I attended a good school, went on holidays every year, rode horses and wore nice clothes. Life was peachy most of the time, but it wasn't all handed on a plate.

At fifteen, I got a part-time job to pay for nights out with friends. I soon learned the value of money, and having to work hard to earn it. I funded my social life, my clothes and any extras I wanted. The deal was I could go out if I paid my own way. I worked in sports shops, cafés and call centres as well as flyering to earn money. I loved feeling like an entrepreneur, independent and grown-up.

My childhood was happy overall; there was nothing obviously wrong. But I was aware of missing memories, and certain ages I couldn't remember anything about. Assuming this was normal, I put it down to a poor memory and accepted it as that. There was no reason to question anything; my life had been good so far. When I accidentally began a healing journey six years ago, I came to understand more about the forgotten memories. I learned about suppressing the past, which we all do to some extent.

Difficult or traumatic experiences (of which we have many) can leave little "scars" in our mind, body and soul, which we don't want to touch.

We humans are remarkably good at blocking out the bad stuff so we don't re-visit. Good in the short term – but it doesn't work forever.

Finding my inner child

All of us have an "inner child" who resides somewhere inside our psyches. This little girl or boy holds on to the past (especially the parts we've erased) and greatly influences how we live our lives today. Gentle excavation with your inner child can help you find the scars and understand more about the adult you are now. She or he knows your history, and holds many answers about why you behave the way you do.

When I discovered my inner child, she had quite a different picture of the childhood I remember. She reminded me about feeling "different" and "unsafe" and that my only wish was to "fit in". She remembered dimming my light, being sensitive to life, and closing myself down to avoid standing out and getting attention. I reflected back to find more answers.

As cool as they are now, my parents were off-the-wall and quite eccentric. They strayed away from the herd to do their own thing. They wore quirky Japanese clothes, drove vintage cars, and bought only organic food. We holidayed in cultural cities rather than chilling at the beach – wholly embarrassing when I was sharing my summer plans with friends who travelled to fun-filled seaside resorts. Everything we did was radical, and in my young impressionable mind, we stuck out. I was trying my best to be "normal" and my parents seemed so alien. While I accept it's natural for parents to be embarrassing, my hyper-awareness of how different we were made me extremely uncomfortable. Among Liverpudlians we looked distinctive, we sounded different, and we did the opposite of everyone else.

School was tough. My uniform was hand-me-down, faded

and musty, with patches at the elbows. I felt (and smelled) like a misfit, and I'm now put off buying vintage for life. My reports were averagely basic, if that's a thing! I was not academic and I barely scraped through. It was hard to focus and my butterfly mind was always getting me into trouble in class.

Packed lunches were cottage cheese sandwiches on rye bread, sesame snap bars and a packet of raisins (I hate raisins to this day) or chunky egg sandwiches that would stink out the classroom and cause complaints. Other kids had white bread, Monster Munch crisps, Penguin bars and a can of Coke. No one ever wanted to swap with me. Who wants a smelly lunch?

I felt like the weird kid in class, and wholeheartedly believed that I stuck out. I felt awkward and unsafe among my classmates, and in my body too. Paranoia was my best friend, and in my mind everyone was talking behind my back. I worried they wouldn't want to be friends. All I ever wanted was to blend in with the crowd, but it wasn't happening. Everything I did drew attention to myself.

I was painfully shy, turning bright red whenever the attention was focused on me. I wanted to stay beneath the radar, and not stick out in any way. I dreaded being questioned in class, as I'd never know the answer; I'd be too busy daydreaming and sun-gazing out the window.

At some point, to save myself and my reputation, I vowed to do the exact opposite to my parents. Rather than stand out, I made it my mission to blend in and be part of the herd. It's safer in numbers, so I knew it'd be better. I longed to be a wallflower and seek refuge in the long grass.

If you know me now it's hard to believe, as I'm loud, gregarious and very sociable, but back then it was very true.

Not being "enough"

Aged around ten, I came out of my shell and decided to change. I suppressed the shyness to relate to the world in a louder, bolder way. Perhaps I was encouraged to speak up more? Perhaps I realised that being shy wouldn't get me where I wanted to go in life? Whatever happened, as I suppressed my shy side, I forgot all about her, and her wish to blend in. She didn't leave me, or change into something else, instead she was pushed into the background and into the shadows.

Along came senior school and I searched for my "tribe", a gang I could happily lose myself in and be absorbed into their personalities. I considered my options and tried out a few for size before finally setting my hopes on the "cool" gang in our year. It wasn't an easy ride as from the get-go some of them didn't want me. I was treated as a threat, and one of the girls worked hard to keep me on the outside. I wasn't invited out after school, they didn't save me seats in class or wait for me after P.E. Despite being rejected a few times, I was still convinced I'd found my "peeps". I clung on like a limpet, desperately waiting for any sign or acknowledgement of being accepted. I'm not sure how or when, but it happened eventually and I became one of them.

Anxiety kicked in. I felt insecure and fragile and, most of all, eager to please and desperate to be liked and accepted. I did everything I could to ensure this happened, but inside I was crumbling. One wrong move and I might be cast out of the gang I'd worked so hard to join. I overanalysed everything: what to say, how I'd sound, what to wear, how to act. I felt sure I wasn't "cool" enough or "funny" enough or "clever" enough. I worried they wouldn't love me for being me.

I was afraid to be me.

The fear was so strong, it was paralysing. It stopped me from being my authentic self and from expressing myself the way I'd have liked to. At times I felt frantic, desperate to be liked and seen, because otherwise I was ignored and rejected, which hurt so much more.

This act of suppressing my true self caused me to feel intense inner pain and rage, and these, in turn, meant I lashed out at the people closest to me. At home I was a petulant teenager who lived in a black hole. I was wild, vicious, untamable (my mum's words, not mine). I spent four years slamming doors, stomping up the stairs and arguing with the rest of the family over dinner – not the most pleasant of times for any of us. I hated the world, and once I was in the midst of an "episode", try as I might I couldn't snap out of it. I kept everything buried deep inside me where it festered and fermented in my gut, making my anger a whole lot worse.

I know I'm not alone in this. In my experience, lots of us believe we're not "enough". This feeling can be especially strong in the teenage years, when we're finding out who we are and comparing ourselves to others, but for many it persists way beyond then and can really start to hold us back in life. Low self-esteem affects relationships, work prospects and general happiness. What's strange is that many people suffering from low self-esteem don't even realise it. They never put into words that somehow they don't feel quite "enough". It took me a long time to realise it myself.

Starting a journey into the past

Experiences in our youth shape the people we become as adults. Some of them we remember, most we don't. The real skill as a human being is to live through experiences, learn from them and grow – but often we get stuck with the learning and growing parts. Most of the values and foundations upon which we've built ourselves were laid down during childhood, so we've been heavily influenced by old memories.

———

Even if we mostly remember happy times, there will have been plenty of times when we felt rejected, abandoned, alone, unloved, and these memories will stick to us like Velcro.

———

Some of us are fiercely protective of our parents, or simply in denial that anything was less than perfect, but in order to move forwards, it's important to be honest with yourself.

Common occurrences that might resonate with you include:

- parents getting divorced or arguing a lot;
- failing exams;
- getting lost in a public place;
- being pushed too hard by parents;
- having an accident or serious illness;
- being rejected by a friendship group;

- a family member's alcoholism;
- losing a parent;
- sexual abuse;
- emotional abuse;
- domestic violence.

Some of these are more serious than others, but it's the way you experienced those events and your innate character that determine how much they affect you as an adult, rather than the severity of the event itself. Some people are more sensitive and hold onto damage more than others.

When we have an experience, good or bad, it's as if we take a Polaroid (an instant picture), freezing the moment and the emotion we felt then, and store it in our subconscious. Over the years this creates a network of "baggage" with a big emotional charge, which lies behind the scenes waiting to be processed and released.

―――

Inner wounds are buried deep underneath our everyday modern woes and cause anxiety, depression, fears, stress, illness, addictive behaviours and self-sabotage.

―――

When the pressure of life gets too much to handle, it's easy for old wounds to be "triggered" and we react from those deeply buried places without even realising that's what we're doing.

I carried my "not good enough" wounds into my adult life as core beliefs about myself. My beliefs created my behaviours, and in my mind I thought I was never doing enough. In meetings, I'd worry about not contributing enough, or having a loud enough voice. I felt constantly insecure and anxious that I'd be singled out, just as I was in school. I played myself down and didn't allow people to see the real me. And if I made a mistake or something went wrong, I'd feel completely ashamed. I'd get paranoid that I was being talked about and was about to be sacked. I'd feel guilty, blamed, and I'd punish myself by working late.

We are skilled at avoiding our emotional baggage, because we've learned how to protect ourselves. If you grew up in a family where you were discouraged from sharing or opening up emotionally, the process will be even harder for you.

But emotional baggage doesn't just vanish. If we don't address it, sooner or later it will spill out and damage our lives and our potential for happiness. That's why it's important to try and reconnect the dots about what situations made us the way we are now.

Buy a notebook to devote to LifeTonics.

When you start writing, let it flow without judgement. Allow yourself to write whatever you want to. When you get stuck, keep writing without taking the pen off the page. No one will read it but you, so be completely honest. And here's what to write about on page one:

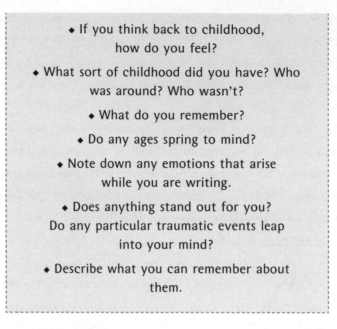

- If you think back to childhood,
  how do you feel?
- What sort of childhood did you have? Who
  was around? Who wasn't?
- What do you remember?
- Do any ages spring to mind?
- Note down any emotions that arise
  while you are writing.
- Does anything stand out for you?
  Do any particular traumatic events leap
  into your mind?
- Describe what you can remember about
  them.

Bringing more awareness to traumatic moments in childhood can help us to understand why we react the way we do in certain situations as adults: why we feel rejected, why we struggle to focus, why we worry so much. Understanding this helps you feel liberated, as you're beginning to set yourself free. Awareness gives us our power back, and helps us heal.

Don't worry about not having all the answers at once; they will come at the right time.

The aim of this book is to help you heal. We'll explore your life together, trying to understand what was really happening back in your childhood and how it affected you in the present day. We'll then move through it and into a brighter, happier life.

There is nothing wrong with you. You've simply experienced

painful things. We all have. But now it's your time to learn and grow.

Learning lessons from the past

As you begin to face your "shadows", the parts you are suppressing, it's common to feel uncomfortable, frustrated, anxious, even scared. It happens all the time – except now you're going to learn from the experience. Life is constantly providing us with opportunities to heal, like a vast, efficient ecosystem, designed to help us grow.

There are three "learnings" I'd like to share at the end of this first chapter.

1) DON'T BLAME THE PARENTS. It's easy to do this. Why weren't they there when I needed them? It's all their fault; they messed up. It's because of their actions my life is such a mess. OK, sure, they let you down, they weren't always there, and those moments of absence hurt. No one is perfect but most parents did the best they possibly could, the way they were shown by their parents (who weren't perfect either). Mine wanted nothing but the best for their children and if the lives we led when I was a child caused me some emotional trauma, it's not their fault. Ultimately, it's point-less holding onto blame. It only hurts you. In order to transform your life, you need to let it go. We'll work on this more in Chapter 27.

2) WE GROW FROM OUR EXPERIENCES. Everything we've ever experienced in our lives has contained a lesson. There is no such thing as a wasted experience. No matter how dark your past, there is a reason why it happened, and ultimately it will make you a stronger person. Some of my clients have been through horrendous experiences, the worst darkness you can imagine, and they emerged through the other side stronger than before. When we learn to be open and process the past, it is possible to make big shifts in a very short space of time.

3) IT'S ALL GOOD IN THE END! It really is. Whatever you're currently facing, however scary it is, you will rise above it a better person, and be much lighter and brighter. Everyone heals at some point. Some scars take a little longer because they have more layers to heal, more teachings to receive and understand. But the more you address and transform, the easier it becomes.

Let's start now, moving onwards and upwards together.

2

Masters of Avoidance

We all have baggage from our past. It doesn't matter if your childhood was delightful and loving or utterly horrific: each one of us has experienced suffering in some way. It's a part of the human experience. The question now is: what do we do about it?

The answer: we find a remedy. Of which, there are several different options available to us. However, the easiest option in life is to avoid the baggage one way or another, and most of us do this. It's easier than confronting the pain, so why wouldn't we?

We live in a fast-paced, workaholic society full of material possessions and chemical substances that can help us numb our pain. We have medicine to mask every kind of symptom, remedies to help us escape from everyday reality and, for a while at least, we can completely avoid our pain if we choose.

We excel in avoidance. Dodging our baggage is much easier than facing it.

Why? Because if we face our baggage, we have to confront our pain. And why on earth would we want to do that? The most effective avoidance is through addictions, which offer a quick fix to plaster over pain from the past.

I bet you £50 that when I mentioned addiction, you immediately thought of hard drugs and homeless people, completely discounting yourself in the process. But there are lots of different types of addiction: shopping (online or in shops), gambling, love, sex, smoking, over- or under-eating, self-harming, work, exercise, alcohol, drugs, computer games, social media. Addiction can be whatever is easily available to us, anything that offers us a short-term fix or temporary high. Anything to distract us from facing ourselves.

Right now you might not even be aware of your addiction. I work with lots of people who are in complete denial. We grow up believing that certain addictive behaviours are a normal part of life. Sometimes we're taught them as children but most often, if you delve deep and get behind the scenes, you'll find emotional trauma attached to old memories at the root of an addiction.

The first step is to become aware, and bring the mindless numbing into the light.

———

"Whatever you do, don't try and escape the pain, but be with it."
– Sogyal Rinpoche

———

I'm not suggesting you're an alcoholic if you enjoy a few glasses of wine some evenings, but if you regularly drink more than the recommended limits (fourteen units a week, or three in one night) and your drinking feels out of control, you might have a problem.

> ### Grab your notebook and do some free writing:
> - ◆ What might your addictions be?
> - ◆ How are you escaping yourself?
> - ◆ What can't you live without?
> - ◆ What are you doing that helps you cope with your hectic lifestyle?
> - ◆ How often do you have a "blow-out"?
> - ◆ Be honest with yourself. It's pointless doing it otherwise.

Do you take illegal drugs? Were you a fan of those party highs that have now become illegal in the UK and many other countries around the world? If you think you have become dependent on drugs or alcohol, seek help from one of the agencies listed on page 262.

Do you sleep with people you really shouldn't? What are you really seeking from those one-night stands?

If you enjoy shopping, great; but if you've got thousands of pounds of debt on credit cards and are always overdrawn, you might have a problem.

Constantly on social media? That's fine, most of us are. But can you go on holiday and switch your phone off? Can you post something and then leave it for a day or two without needing to check the number of "likes"?

Use your common sense. What are you "using" in your life to numb your pain and escape from yourself?

Masking deeper issues

Addictions always hide a deeper issue – or several deeper issues. The old baggage, pain, emotion, trauma from your past has been stuffed so far down it's completely out of reach. Because you don't want to address this anytime soon, the easiest solution is to keep on stuffing it down. Except this pit is inside you, and everything in it begins to fester sooner or later. If you don't deal with it, it'll come out in other ways.

What would happen if you faced yourself and stopped running? I've done this, so believe me when I say I know what it's like.

My main addiction was bulimia, which I battled for seven years. Although when I say "battled" it's not strictly true because it felt quite normal. My binge-eating and purging sessions always went smoothly, and I never stopped to think about what I was actually doing to myself. It was a part of me, but unseen and well hidden. Nobody knew anything about it.

The frequency and intensity of the bulimia depended on what I was battling in my life at the time. When things felt wobbly and out of control, it worsened. When things were calm and relaxed, it subsided. It was always there, though, tapping me on my shoulder, offering me a way out. Whenever I needed a fix I could always turn to it.

As with most addicts, I became very good at keeping it secret. I hid my bulimia so well, I was in denial about it. If you somehow peeked inside my brain, you'd find zero trace because I'd become very good at removing all the evidence. If I was ever asked about my eating habits, I gazed blankly into the distance. I was busy living my life, and my secret was buried so deep inside I just didn't recognise I had a problem.

And of course I'm not alone. A huge percentage of us have had some kind of issue with food and our bodies. I don't think I've met one person who hasn't. It's one of the main areas we have control over in our lives.

As far as my friends and family knew, I was totally fine: the life and soul of a party, and a tough cookie. The thing is, I'm genetically wired to struggle on as bravely as possible (preferably alone) and not show any weakness or vulnerability in the process.

My history of binge eating starts at the family dinner table. We were definitely "eaters" and loved big portions. We'd pile our plates high, and eat everything on them. Mum loved seeing us eat everything in sight, and knew her job was done when we had. Ever the big tease, Dad would pretend to steal food from our plates when we weren't looking. It was a fun game, and I soon became able to eat just as fast and as much as him so he wouldn't have a chance. I accidentally learned about overeating when I was very young. This is apparently very common. It's easy to ignore the signs that your stomach is full, and keep eating.

And then one day my body changed. I didn't suddenly become big or fat overnight; I just needed to monitor my weight and do more exercise. I remember an ex-boyfriend telling me that I'd be even better if I lost a few pounds. I was seventeen and a healthy weight for my age, but his comment stuck with me.

Fast forward six years and the bulimia started. After witnessing how easy it was, I kept doing it. For me, it was the perfect solution to eating too much and putting on weight. I could now eat whatever I wanted without it affecting my body image or happiness. I was pretty pleased with myself. No one would ever know, unless I wanted them to. I could stay small, look good in my clothes, and be known as the skinny one.

Stuffing down food became a way to stuff down my emotions. To keep them suppressed deep inside, out of my way. If only I could keep pushing them all down forever, I could easily breeze through life – or so I thought. My mind was completely behind this idea; its primary focus was to keep me safe and protected no matter what, so it latched on, removed all "stop eating" signs and helped me to become an addict.

Deep down I was crying out for help, but I couldn't connect to my desperation. You have to delve down quite far to find the part of you that is scared, anxious and freaked out by life being so out of control. You are desperate to claw back control, and you grasp at straws trying to figure out why you're so full of fear. Why does life frighten you so much? How can you gain some normality and feel safe again? You do whatever you can to get a grip.

What I see now is that overeating was my addiction, and bulimia was my way of dealing with it. Overeating becomes an addiction quickly because it really works. It was my default way of dealing with life, just as getting high on drugs is for some people, or drinking until they are hopelessly drunk and distracted from what's really going wrong.

If, as you're reading this, your addiction is slowly – or rapidly – unravelling before your eyes and you feel scared: don't be. My message to you is that you're reading this for a reason, and it's unravelling at just the right time for you to do something about it. You're courageous for picking up this book, and now you are beginning a process of becoming more aware. This is just the first step. You don't have to tell anyone else what you are discovering. For now, it is just about accepting it yourself.

We hold onto things, and keep them a secret because we don't know how to deal with them at the time. We can't see how to move forwards because we know that in doing so, we might be required to face some painful memories. We're not ready to face that pain yet, and that is absolutely OK. There's a chance that this chapter is the main reason you were guided to read this book. Maybe it has found you at just the right time.

Whatever you're facing right now, know that you are an amazing person and truly good inside. The best thing you can do is tell yourself this. No matter what you're feeling, or how sad you are, there's a little inner child or teenager deep inside you who is hurting more than you know. In the next step, you are going to find them and comfort them and tell them that everything will be OK. Because it will.

For a moment, sit somewhere quiet, close your eyes and connect with your inner child or teenager. Choose the age you identified in the last chapter at which you felt most vulnerable, the time when you felt the most pain. If you didn't come up with a specific age, what age do you get now? Taking it slow and steady, intend to speak to the person you were at that age and tell him or her this:

I see you.
(Pause and repeat)

I feel you.
(Pause and repeat)

I sense you.
(Pause and repeat)

I'm sorry I wasn't there for you.
But I'm here now.
(Pause and repeat)

How does it feel when you say these words?

Is there anything else you want to say to them?
Do any other words come up for you?

Notice how your body feels.
Does it tense up? Does it relax?

You are stronger than you know. You have a feisty inner self who is always rooting for you – and so am I! This inner self will never give up, and if you ask it for help, you will receive it, without question.

CHAPTER

—⟨3⟩—

Spirits and Signs

Do you believe in the supernatural?

Saying that word sends shivers down my spine, in a good way. It reminds me of those seriously sexy and ultra-cool vampire movies like *The Lost Boys*, *Blade* and, most recently *Twilight* (my guilty crush). As a child, I was fascinated with vampires, spirits and witches. When I was very little, I'd watch back-to-back episodes of *Bewitched*, and developed a nose twitch like Samantha's. It's something I still do to this day, usually a sign that something is awry.

I was always aware of the presence of spirits in the old house in Liverpool where I grew up. I'd notice if the temperature dropped suddenly or the dog barked at an empty room. At nighttime, I was afraid of being downstairs alone in case I saw something spooky. The house was old and creaky, and its walls were steeped in history. I knew every squeak, every thump, every smell – especially the ones that didn't belong.

Not a believer in spirits? Please don't skip this chapter! Suspend your disbelief for a few minutes and try to be open-minded. I'm sure you'll agree there's much we can't explain, or can't see with the naked eye. Once you are willing to accept the possibility of a supernatural realm, you become more open to things of this nature happening to you, and in my experience there's nothing to fear. In fact, we can learn to receive guidance, messages and reassurance from the spirit world. Most of all, we can gain a deeper under-standing of death and the afterlife, and put aside our fear of it.

We are energy. Yes, we're skin, bones, tissue, muscles, cells, but we're also "spiritual" energy. It flows through the body's energy meridian lines throughout our constitution. Our words are energy, as are the emotions we feel, our thoughts and our actions. Spiritual energies exist around us too, and some of these are called "spirit guides".

Imagine you have a collective of guides or helpers all around you with your best interests at heart.

Included in these are family members and friends who have passed away. I discovered the truth of this for myself back in 2004 and it blasted open my mind, and my heart . . .

Up close and personal

I dated Sam (not his real name) while I was in Liverpool during a year out from uni. He had an air of innocence about him. His energy felt pure, light and angelic. Despite this, he told me about several brushes with the law he'd had in the past, and how lucky he'd been to escape unscathed. We had lots of fun together but

I always knew the relationship would end when I went back to uni in Manchester. It didn't seem long-term. To me, he was a best friend whom I loved dearly and we were very close. As I expected we broke up when I went back to uni but Sam kept in touch and we remained close friends.

One weeknight in March 2004, he called and told me his car tyres had been slashed with a knife outside a bar near his house. As I listened, shivers ran up and down my spine, and I immediately turned ice-cold. I told him to be careful, to watch his back. He assured me he was fine, that it must have been a mix-up in which the wrong person had been targeted. I relaxed a little, and we hung up.

A couple of weeks later, I called him. The phone rang out then went through to voicemail. I left a message and expected to hear from him later because he always called me back. But a couple of days passed and I heard nothing. I thought it was odd, but I brushed it off and buried myself back in my books.

The next day I was in a lecture when my phone started ringing. I looked down to see it was a friend calling, but I couldn't take the call. She proceeded to call me five times in a row, so I knew it was something urgent. I went outside and called her back, and she told me she had to see me later that day. I wasn't keen because I had so much work to do, but she persisted. I figured that something had happened to her, so I caved in and arranged to meet back at my house.

Some time later, her car pulled up outside. I opened the door, she came inside and straight away told me to sit down. Then she told me that Sam had been involved in an accident, and he was dead. She continued, saying that he'd been stabbed by an ex-best friend of his from school. It all happened in broad daylight on a street outside a primary school. I was so stunned, I couldn't speak and I went into deep shock. My friend drove me home to Liverpool, to my parents' house.

That first night back at home, I didn't sleep in my own bed but crept into my brother's room (he was away) and slept in his. Everything was still and quiet. I was empty and exhausted with grief. Just as I was falling asleep, I felt a calming, peaceful energy surrounding me, and the room suddenly changed. It was enough to make me sit up, and as I did so, I saw a powerful outline of Sam sitting on the bed, bathed in a glow of light. His head was in his hands, and I sensed he was struggling. I had the insight that he was torn between staying in this world and moving on to the next (although I wasn't sure what that meant).

I'd never had an experience like this before, yet I knew with absolute certainty it was Sam. I went into autopilot, and told him we were all OK, that it was time for him to go, and that we all loved him and we understood. Moments later he was gone, and the room was restored to the way it had been before. I felt very lucky that I'd seen him one last time, that I could feel he was OK and that he was going somewhere peaceful. It gave me some relief from the terrible pain of the loss.

Eleven years later, my granny passed away, and I knew the instant it happened. She'd been ill and I could feel she was suffering. I got a text from my brother, telling me the ambulance had been called. Suddenly an image of Granny came into my mind. I could sense she was struggling to let go of her life, that she was afraid to leave us because she'd been the matriarch and headed up the family (or so she thought).

Without her, would we be OK? She didn't want to leave us exposed. I told her we'd be fine and it was time for her to go. We loved her and were so grateful for all her support. I said goodbye, and an hour later she died peacefully.

And I haven't lost either of them because they're now my spirit guides. Whenever I have a decision to make, or I'm doing something complicated, I always sense them around, encouraging me and telling me to keep going. It's lovely and comforting.

We are all connected with each other, even when we've passed away.

You can "ask" to connect with anyone who has passed. Perhaps there was something you didn't get to say to them while they were alive? Do you have regrets about what you didn't say before they passed away? There's still time.

> *Write a letter to any deceased loved ones you think you'd like to connect with. Writing activates your subconscious mind (where your pain is stored) so will support you as you release old pain. Go through this process for each person you feel you want to talk to:*
>
> **1)** Find a quiet space with a desk and chair. Get a writing pad and a nice pen, and light a scented candle next to you.

2) Before you write anything, close your eyes and take some deep breaths. Put your hand over your heart and feel the breath going into your heart as you inhale. Imagine the person you are writing to in your mind and heart. Even if you can't see them, the intention to connect with them is enough. Stay with your feelings, or with any emotions that come up. Release these emotions gently, and give yourself the space to grieve a little more.

3) Next, take your pen and pad. Write a letter and allow the words to flow, writing down whatever's on your mind. Tell them how sorry you were they passed away, or how much you wished you'd said you loved them before they died. Tell them what you want them to know about your life now. Say whatever is on your mind. Even if you find it upsetting, this is a beautiful healing exercise.

Message from a medium

Five years after Sam died I went to visit a psychic medium (someone who connects with spirits or ghosts or energies that are living with us in this reality or that come to visit us from the supernatural realm). Soon after the session began, the room turned icy cold. Suddenly, Sam appeared and I could feel him standing behind me. Through the medium, Sam gave me accurate information about what his family looked like, and messages to give them about his welfare. There's no way the medium would know his family, nor about what had happened, so it got my full attention. He also told me to let him go, which I remember thinking was odd because I believed I had already let him go. But he was right; I was still holding on to guilt because I hadn't been there when he needed me. He told me he'd always be guiding me wherever I went in life. And my favourite piece of advice of all: he told me to watch out for signs. He told me I'd be spiritually guided by angels, and to listen to anyone who came into my path with an important message to share. He said that I'd know intuitively what this meant, and I'd be told to listen clearly when this happened.

This experience opened my senses to the supernatural, and afterwards I felt less afraid of death. Spiritual experiences help us to gain a new understanding about the afterlife. We live on, not in physical form but through our souls or legacies, and we might then help to guide others.

I can feel Sam's presence with me now, as a guide, an angel and a guardian.

Have you lost anyone close to you? The pain can be excruciating, depending on the circumstances surrounding their death. But I believe they never truly leave us and that they are still around in a way we don't fully understand. Awareness of this presence can give us comfort as we confront the challenges of everyday life, and support as we go through the process of becoming more self-aware and opening up our inner emotional "baggage" to the light of day.

Living Life to the Extreme

Life in the 21st century is super-fast-paced and it's easy to feel as if you're on a treadmill, running endlessly ahead without actually getting anywhere. Maybe you're working flat out to pay rent or a mortgage or to raise children. Perhaps you're stuck in an unfulfilling job you can't afford to give up. Maybe all those dreams you used to have as a child or a teenager have been thrown away because they'd be too difficult to achieve, or you don't think you are capable or you've convinced yourself it couldn't happen. Have you "settled" for a life that is all hard slog with few rewards?

Lots of us plug ourselves into a fast-paced life, without realising that our light is dimmed and our spirit is starved.

When we're chasing things, searching outside for answers, hits or fixes, we ignore our need to nourish our inner light, our spirit. We forget about its existence as we bury ourselves deeper into work and/or partying. But sooner or later, the burden and stress of this kind of life brings all our fears to the surface. Before long you'll crack under the pressure and your inner "baggage" will start leaking out. There is no escape, not really. Whatever relief we feel before the cracks start to appear is temporary. Our minds create the illusion of escape to keep us safe and protected.

Trying to free yourself from this endless treadmill of life is hard, because of lack of time, lack of money, lack of self-belief. In this chapter I'm going to suggest ways you can step off the treadmill and move towards a life that will nourish you both inside and out. And first I'll share my own experiences of the mistakes I made before I finally found my own true path.

Life in the fast lane

During my twenties, I worked in an ad agency in London and partied hard most nights. Life was full of extremes and self-destruction. I was doing everything I could to avoid facing myself. I was riding a high-speed train and I clung on for dear life, thinking that if I kept moving fast enough I would be fine. What other choice did I have? I didn't know any different.

For ten long years, I was a square peg in a round hole, kidding myself that advertising was the perfect job for me. Being a "yes" person, I was soon working twelve-hour days without a lunch break. The days were full of back-to-back meetings, long and late client calls, collisions with scary creative directors and a laughable work-hard, play-hard mentality.

I felt inadequate when I compared myself to everyone else. I wasn't half as good as them; I wasn't qualified or experienced enough. How had I got here? Had my bosses made a mistake when they hired me? I lived in fear of being "found out", convincing myself I was about to be sacked. I tossed and turned at night, a black cloud of impending doom ever present in my dreams. Burned-out and running on empty, I was always the last one in the office because I never felt I'd achieved enough to leave on time. On Friday night I'd stay for drinks in order to blot out all feelings of unworthiness that lingered in the background. Over the weekend I'd go out partying, bury myself in the scene, get high and then feel guilty. Come Sunday I'd be sobbing into my pillow and wishing the ground would swallow me up.

I'd created a cycle of destruction. I couldn't handle the pressure so I'd use partying as a release, which then brought on guilt. To punish myself, I'd work even harder in my job, beating myself up to make amends for going wild. It was a vicious circle that was only heading one way. But when you're stuck in the middle, it's hard to find your way out, and sometimes it takes a complete change of scene.

Playing hard

I always loved dancing, from when I was just fourteen years old. Going out clubbing fed my soul, and the memories still do: the bright lights, the dry ice and the dance floor. I loved a good party, and thrived on being right in among it. I loved nothing more than letting my hair down and having a blow-out.

I was hooked on the way I felt on the dance floor. Goosebumps would rise on my skin, my hair would stand on end, and certain tunes would awaken something deep inside. My spirit would emerge, and for a few moments she felt strong and alive – until I numbed her with alcohol.

One year I went on holiday to Ibiza, the ultimate party island, and it seemed life made more sense under sunny skies. I worked out there for two seasons in some of the best clubs and made a load of friends who were into the same things as me. It was a good life for a while, but ultimately it was still about escaping. I had perfected the art of escapism, running away from my old "baggage" from the past and my deep, negative inner feelings and thoughts. I wanted to numb myself by diverting my attention fully and deeply into some thing else. It wasn't the answer – it was just another form of avoidance.

I still wasn't getting any kind of creative fulfilment. I was no closer to finding out who I really was and what my talents were.

I'm not suggesting that partying is bad, or going to the pub after work is a no-go. But when you are doing it to escape pain, it can quickly lead to unhealthy addictive behaviours. As we have seen, to move forwards you have to face up to the baggage you are carrying around, dig deep to look at its causes, learn the lessons and grow.

> *Time to get your LifeTonic journal out again, and start writing whatever comes into your head about your ideal job.*
>
> ◆ Can you remember what you wanted to be when you were a child of about eight? And then what about when you were twelve? And sixteen?
>
> ◆ How do you feel about your current job? What do you like about it and what would you like to change?
>
> ◆ What's your dream job? If money was taken out of the equation, how would you like to spend your working life?

As soon as you have admitted your dream job, I bet you are thinking of all the reasons why you couldn't possibly do it. You'd have to go back to college or uni to retrain. You'd be scared to give up a confirmed salary for the insecurity of freelance life. You don't think you are good enough to make it a success.

Now I want you to take the fear out of this equation and brainstorm ways you could start taking steps towards achieving your dream. Could you study part-time, or in evening school? Could you earmark a few hours every weekend to focus on what you really want to do? Who do you know who could help you? Jot down some ideas.

If you had told me back in the Ibiza days that I would one day be writing a book advising people on how to be their best selves, I'd have thought you were crazy. Me? Write a book? Or have anything worth saying in it? And yet, here we are . . .

Don't self-sabotage

As you set out on the path to finding your perfect career, something to nourish and light you up, be mindful of any blocks that might get in the way. Self-doubt is one of the biggest, and fear of failure is a close ally. We can get stuck in a cycle of self-sabotage because of our deep fear of failure. And when it doesn't work out, we say to ourselves "I told you so!" Our little negative voice pipes up and succeeds at keeping us stuck and small.

There are lots of different methods of self-sabotage: taking drugs, drinking too much, over-eating and all the other types of harmful behaviour we discussed in Chapter 3, turning up late for a job interview because you couldn't decide what to wear, or you left it till the last minute then the train was delayed; not finishing your uni coursework because a friend wanted to talk about her new boyfriend; not starting to write that novel because the kids need you to be a 24/7 mum. There are lots of excuses you can make about why you haven't tried to achieve your dreams, but instead of calling them "excuses" why not think of them as "self-sabotage". They are undermining you in your journey.

Make the decision to help yourself and put the focus on you. It's tough as first, but far more rewarding in the long term.

5

Waking Up

If you've read this far without fully opening yourself up to the processes I'm describing, it's absolutely fine. The time has to be right for us to make fundamental life changes, especially ones that bring deeply buried emotional pain to the surface. I believe that you are searching for something, because you picked up this book and have got this far. Sometimes it takes a sign from the universe to give us a wake-up call and remind us that life as we know it is short and we owe it to ourselves to be happy. The process is scary, though, so keep reading and something will rise up to show you the way to go.

In my own life, the signs from the universe were appearing, but I wasn't very good at seeing them. I knew I didn't want to work in advertising in London, but I couldn't spend my whole life clubbing on a party island either. I reached burn-out in my late twenties. The party lifestyle didn't excite me as much as it once had. The buzz I used to get from a night out was now overshadowed by a raging hangover and heaps of guilt about my behaviour the night before. At work I was sketchy and unproductive.

One morning, lying in bed recovering from a particularly frenetic week, I recognised that the hazy days of partying were drawing to a close. As I realised this, I felt a shift, as if some space was being created. A part of my soul began to stir. Suddenly I felt a yearning for adventure, a deep inner urge to go somewhere far away. I let my mind wander, thinking of all the places I might go, and before long I had settled on South America. Some of my friends had been a few years earlier, and it sounded like a special place. I already had a friend living out there, and everything I'd heard about it sounded radical and unique. My heart lit up, as an inner light flicked on. I could sense myself coming alive, as I knew instantly it was the right decision. My skin shivered as I got ready to make this trip of a lifetime. I handed in my notice at work, booked a plane ticket, packed my backpack and off I went.

---

*"Look deep into nature, and
then you will understand everything better."
– Albert Einstein*

A special plant

Travelling from country to country was eye-opening, as each place offered something completely unique and amazing. At first it was all a bit overwhelming but by the time I reached Brazil, I was feeling more confident, which was convenient because it was alive with culture and so much bigger than I'd expected. Being in Rio for Carnival was a memorable and deeply moving experience.

While exploring northeast Brazil, I heard about a retreat centre deep in the jungle of Peru that offered healing through special plants. It was run by indigenous shamans from a tribe known as the Shipibo. Straight away I felt a powerful resonance, as if my soul knew this was part of the "plan" and I had to go. I visited the website and the more I read about this place, the more I felt drawn to it. They promised to detox the body, and offer profound spiritual insights through the use of ayahuasca, a psychoactive 'brew' made from two plants – the ayahuasca vine and the leaf of the chacruna plant (DMT). Both are collected from the jungle to create a potent mixture that offers access to the realm of spirits and an energetic world that we are usually unable to perceive in our ordinary state of consciousness as normal human beings. It rids the body of physical impurities, negative energies, deep-seated emotional problems and fear-filled beliefs. People who had been through the experience described feeling as if they had been reborn; they said their true purpose in life came to them, and that's exactly what I was looking for.

It wouldn't be easy. For two weeks before visiting the retreat, I had to follow a strict diet, avoiding sugar, salt, alcohol, meat, dairy, coffee, food additives and several other things, so there would be no more nice restaurants. I met some people who had taken ayahuasca, and they described it as having the worst taste you could possibly imagine and told me that it makes you vomit continuously, but still I was determined to try. I was up for changing my life and everything I heard about the retreat sounded as though it would be a good experience for me.

A few months later I arrived at the Temple of the Way of the Light centre in a clearing in the Peruvian jungle. I was greeted by some of the Shipibo people, who beamed at me while chattering away in their native tongue. They had long, thick, ebony hair and big smiles. They dressed in brightly coloured, long-sleeved blouses with frills around the collarbone, black skirts and no shoes. After the introductions, I was assessed by a shaman and given a strict schedule for the next twelve days. There were herbal detox potions to cleanse my digestive system, lots of rituals to perform, and before long I was attending my first ayahuasca ceremony.

Nothing could have prepared me for that first taste of the ayahuasca medicine. It looked like chocolate mousse but was a thick, gloopy mixture full of lumps that made me gag. It tasted like tree bark, a little sour, a bit salty, with an aftertaste that reminded me of Marmite. After finishing my cup, I lay back on my cushion and before long I started having intense experiences: voices chattering in my head, a feeling as though I was being cradled in the arms of a wise mother pouring love into me. My heart was bursting as I opened up to the amazing sense of love and healing I felt, and all the negative memories from my past gushed out in a rapid flow. Later, I experienced the vomiting I'd been told about but despite that, and the foul taste, I couldn't wait to go through my next ayahuasca ceremony.

At the end of a ceremony several nights into my stay, one

of the Shipibo women came over, bent down next to me and hugged me. Then, several other Shipibos followed her. They all gathered around me and started calling me "doctor" in Shipibo and repeating it over and over. They were smiling and laughing with me, as if I was one of them. It was a very clear message: they somehow knew that I was destined to be a healer like them and they could see my future before I could. It was the most surreal experience of my life, and I knew that whatever was happening was very, very special.

By the time I left the jungle I had no doubt what my future calling was. I had been healed from deep within by these Shipibo people and their magical jungle plants, and now I realised that I had to do the same for other people. This was what my life would be devoted to.

How can you find your true path?

I am not recommending that you raid your savings and book a flight to Peru to take part in an ayahuasca ceremony. There have been reports in the media of some corrupt shamans taking advantage of tourists who fly out to experience the effects of the medicine, and at least one tourist is said to have died after taking ayahusaca. It's a shame because my own experience was very pure and profound, but I suppose there are other centres where this is not the case.

There are plenty of ways to have your own moment of enlightenment without travelling halfway round the world to get it. If you are open to signs, you will find them. Here are some suggestions:

◆ Spend time on your own in a beautiful, wild place: a
cottage by the seaside or in remote hills, perhaps. Go out
for long walks every day, watching the light on the water
or trees, the different shades of green in the grass or
bushes, the patterns in the clouds. Retreat inside yourself
while keeping your mind open to all thoughts that pop
into it. Take along a journal and write down whatever
you are thinking about. Stay there for at least a week,
longer if possible, living very simply, with no alcohol, no
phones or screens of any kind. Eat simple, natural food,
drink lots of water and let your mind drift. I promise you
will definitely come back with some new ideas about
your role in the world.

◆ On pages 260-1 you'll find a list of books I recommend you
read and links to motivational speakers I have found
inspiring. Have a look and see if any of them appeal. Your
eye might be drawn to one or another for no conscious
reason. Just go with it and try out that speaker or author.
Perhaps they have something to say to you. If you notice a
poster advertising a speaker coming to your town, there
could be a reason why you walked that particular way and
happened to glance up at that exact poster. Be alert for
signs and the universe will show you what you should do.

◆ Sometimes serious illness, either your own or that of
someone close to you, can remind you how short life is
and, in turn, help you to focus on what you want to
achieve while you are here. Volunteering to work for a

charity helping those who are terminally ill is a rewarding experience that can cast a light on your own life. Spending time with old people and asking them about their memories – the high points and low points of their lives – can also be inspiring. Do they have any regrets? Any advice they would pass on from the wisdom of their years? What do you want to have achieved by the time you reach their age and are getting close to the end of your current life? How can you achieve it?

◆ Creativity can be a way to access your inner self: painting, writing for fun, sculpting, making things . . . all of these can guide you to your inner world.

◆ While you are going through the discovery process, write down your dreams every morning when you wake up. You may find they have some insights and messages for you.

The first step is to start listening to your instincts and watching out for signs the universe is sending to you. If you seek help in the right way (i.e. not through alcohol or hard drugs or over-eating or any other escape mechanism such as the ones I described earlier), then you will find it.

6

Relationships 101

Relationships are . . . [Insert your own word(s) here: rewarding/
life-enhancing/fun/tricky/non-existent/traumatic/frustrating/
scary/a minefield/painful/ incredible growth opportunities].

Whichever word(s) you chose represents your own past
experiences of relationships, or perhaps your current experience.

Personally, I've been pulled apart, betrayed, reduced to an
insecure mess, lied to, cheated on and, most of all, pushed
inwards to find myself.

I've lost love, gained love, travelled the world for love, lied
for love, denied love and lost myself in love. I wouldn't do it
all again but, as I look back now, I understand more about
the relationships I've been in. I've forgiven those who hurt me,
released the guilt of hurting them and I've healed my wounds.
I'm honestly grateful for every single second because I've
learned so much about myself.

Everything I felt in the past – the insecurity, fear of rejection,
feeling of being abandoned, believing I wasn't enough and the
constant emotional turmoil – all came from my deep inner

pain and the negative beliefs I held about relationships. I used drink to escape my discomfort. I'd go out, get blind drunk and party away the pain. I dodged my issues easily, and pretended they didn't exist. I behaved badly, and I didn't treat my partners with the respect they deserved. At the slightest sign of rocky roads ahead, I'd be off.

I was great at pointing the finger, blaming my partner and hiding my wounded self. I'd project my inner pain onto them. We all do this and we don't see it, usually because we're in denial.

We'll do anything we can to protect ourselves, because we're afraid of being hurt again as we were in the past.

What about you?

Has your heart been broken many times? Are you the walking wounded?

Are you struggling to find love? Does it seem like you'll be forever single?

Relationships have complex dynamics, and they affect us all differently. In them we thrive and grow, and that process is often painful. We learn lots about ourselves. Even bad relationships are crucial for our self-development journey in life. We're hard-wired for connection, so deep down that's what we all yearn for.

Understanding your relationship patterns

Imagine that we create our reality and everything we see, hear and feel in the outside world. We're attracting people and experiences that respond to the signals from our thoughts, beliefs and feelings. We're constantly sending out information to the universe, and the universe reflects this back to us. In this way, we're creating our relationships and choosing the people who match us at the time.

Except that the information we send out is based on experiences from all past relationships, including those with our parents. Consider all the negativity and pain you have been through, then understand that it is all being projected out into the universe along with your deepest desires. We aren't conscious of the information we're sending out, until we realise the same types of situation keep coming into our space. How annoying!

We continue attracting the same guys or girls who dump on us in the same way, and cause us the same pain. We pull in the same experiences over and over to remind us of our pain, and we beat ourselves up yet again.

Whether we realise it or not (most don't) we are inviting in these people who reject us and cause us pain. I know this might be hard to hear but it's the truth. And the faster we become open to understanding what's really going on, the faster we can move through it and heal ourselves.

We have to look inside ourselves to find the answers. With a bit of thought and emotional honesty we can discover why and how we're creating these negative experiences in our outside world. We can then become more aware, and change our relationship and life experiences. Fast.

> **Take out your LifeTonic notebook and do some free writing. Here are some thoughts to get you started:**
>
> ◆ What do your past relationships have in common?
>
> ◆ What are your patterns? Do you tend to feel insecure and fear rejection? Do you push other people away? Are you the one who finishes relationships or is it more often your partner?
>
> ◆ Are you falling for the same type of person? What three adjectives would you use to describe your general 'type'?
>
> ◆ Can you see how you sabotage your relationships?
>
> ◆ If you have been single for a long time, can you see how you might be pursuing partners who are not the right match for you? Or falling for people who are unavailable in some way (already in a relationship or busy dealing with their own troubles)? This is a way of avoiding emotional pain.

If you had a secure childhood where you felt well loved, you generally grow up to be a confident adult who considers themselves worthy of love. If you had a difficult childhood or have been badly hurt in previous relationships, your self-esteem can be damaged and you may find yourself continually anxious with a new partner, and constantly needing reassurance that they won't leave you. But the more anxious you get, the more they back away, so it becomes a self-fulfilling prophecy.

One way to break these old patterns is to become more aware of them, and be mindful when you choose your next partner. Try to unlock whatever it was in your past that has made you behave the way you do in relationships now. How has your pattern been affected by the baggage you identified in Chapter 1? Can you see the connections? Understanding is the first step towards bringing awareness to your pattern, and being able to change it next time: choosing a person who gives you what you need to thrive, and being able to give them what they need too.

Here's what I've learned from my (many) relationships:

+ **Relationships are the best and fastest way to grow as a person.** Your lover is like a mirror, constantly reflecting back the wounded parts that you've disowned because you don't want to deal with them. This will trigger emotional responses that provide big clues about which part of you needs attention. If you are able to unravel them, they will help you to grow.

◆ **To get the most out of relationships you must be willing to let yourself be vulnerable.** It's part and parcel of being in a couple. When you allow yourself to be more open, you invite the other person to do the same. Great things happen when you let yourself truly be "seen".

◆ **The slow burners make long-term fireworks.** At times you'll hear friends talk about instant attractions, whirlwind romances, mind-blowing sex, burning desires, incredible lovers who swept them off their feet, whisked them off to the Maldives and proposed after six months. Perhaps you've experienced this yourself. Some people get addicted to the high of the whirlwind but these couples usually tend to break up just as quickly as they got together. When people "fall in love" so quickly, they are not truly seeing each other but are imagining they've found their ideal person. They project all the qualities they've been looking for in a partner onto this other person. Once reality hits after a few weeks or months, the comedown can be hard. Relationships take time and effort, and it's usually the slow burners that make the most incredible long-term loves.

◆ **Never, ever try to change another person.** You'll only face resistance and frustration, and rightly so. You can perhaps change a few small annoying habits, but you'll never change the fundamental person. All you can do is change the way you respond to them. Ask yourself whether you are trying to change them to accommodate your own insecurities. Is it because you can't stand looking at your own pain? Instead learn to accept yourself and your "shadows" (the parts of you that are not, as yet, healed) and your relationship will flourish.

◆ **Be grateful for all that you learn about yourself.**
Relationships are huge gifts. They can show you where
your pain points are, and how you've been programmed
to react a certain way. Get clear on these, and you
vastly improve your life. What better gift could there be
than that?

Soulmates

The concept of a "soulmate" has been romanticised so much
by books and films, glossy magazines and TV dramas that it
might seem unobtainable for the average person. It's an inter-
esting term with many interpretations, and perhaps means
something slightly different to everyone. With the desire to find
our "soulmate" comes a fear that if we don't manage it, we'll
live a sad existence.

There's something very special about meeting a kindred
spirit, someone with whom you have a very special connection,
and it's something to be treasured. But I believe we have many
soulmates – family, friends, lovers, teachers and these people
will join you in your life at the right time. Some might stay
with you for a lifetime, some for a few months. It's healthy to
widen your understanding of the term "soulmates", so you'll
attract more of them into your life.

———

*Soulmates definitely come into our lives to help us
grow.*

———

Sometimes this means they'll trigger a reaction from us, opening up raw feelings, emotions, and old pain. Often they'll lift us up to a higher plane, teach us expansion and how to be unconditionally loving. As we're all on this planet to grow, soulmates provide unique opportunities.

You might already recognise the soulmates in your life.

◆ Are there certain souls you feel close to? As if you've known them for lifetimes?

◆ Write a list of the people who nourish you, then think about how you are nourishing your relationships with them. Could you do more?

◆ Every soulmate relationship should be treasured as the unique and precious gift it is.

My own relationship journey

As I said, my relationship pattern in my twenties was definitely to hold back and avoid vulnerability at any cost, and this meant I ran away at the first signs of trouble. I was about to break up with one particular guy when the book *Men Are from Mars, Women Are from Venus*, by John Gray, fell into my lap. I started reading and it made complete sense. I understood how I was pushing my partner away without even realising it. This discovery directed me inwards and I began to understand that I was projecting my own inner pain onto the relationship. Everything I'd been feeling – the insecurity, fear of rejection, believing I wasn't enough, constant emotional turmoil – had come from deep inside me, not him. He had his own baggage, of course, but now I could clearly see what was mine.

I worked on myself, owned my pain, and when I turned back towards the relationship I could sense I was supposed to be there. Despite the low points, the destructive rows and the thoughts of walking away, I managed to stay firmly put with this particular guy. There's a force that pulls us back together if we wander away from each other. It's always there, even when I've let go of the relationship.

Now I'm on an amazing path with an incredible person. It's been far from perfect (I'm sure he won't mind me saying that) but it's been the most transformative experience of my life. He knows my innermost fears, my deepest secrets and my rawest wounds. We know each other's pain points intimately, and have the utmost respect for each other's healing journey. There's a feeling that we'll always work things out, and nothing's too big for us to handle. He's kind and caring, and the most gentle of souls. As my rock, he anchors me while I expand outwards, unfazed by the speed of my journey and my need to travel, work weekends, work on myself.

I hope that your new understanding of yourself will help you to invite in a good match next time or, if you're already with a good person, to nurture and appreciate what you have.

7

Your True Purpose

Have you found your "thing"?

The dream path that excites you, gives you meaning and purpose and feeds your spirit? That fuels you up, energises your system and helps you thrive? That thing you're proud of sharing?

It might be your job, but it doesn't feel like work. It's the thing you are passionate about, that lights up your world?

In other words, your "calling", which might still be out there waiting to be discovered. In this chapter we're going to look at ways of finding your life's true purpose by listening to and observing signs that the universe is sending you.

Your true purpose could mean a change of career, perhaps starting your own business rather than working for someone else. It could mean finding a way to express your creativity. It could mean volunteering in a refugee camp in some wartorn part of the world or working in an animal refuge. The possibilities are endless.

Do you feel like you're not living your true purpose? Is there a little niggle within telling you that there's something else?

Do you often feel exhausted? This can be a clue because when we're stuck in something that no longer serves us, we're moving against our natural flow. We use extra energy to push against the resistance, so we feel overtired.

As part of the process of healing yourself, in this book you are learning to be more attuned to the universe. In this chapter, I want to tell you about listening to your inner voice (in other words, your intuition), trusting what it is saying, recognising and learning from people who have something to teach you and responding to the signs you are given.

Inner voices

After my South American travels, I came back to an office job in London. The Shipibo people telling me I should be a healer had been exciting at the time, but in the cold light of the UK I couldn't think how I could possibly earn a living from it. What would I do? I had no training, no qualifications in any healing profession, and I couldn't afford to go back to uni and study something new. I started taking courses in a few areas that interested me, including Light Grids (an energy and emotional healing technique with meditation – see page 261), Emotional Freedom Technique (EFT) and Reiki (a technique for promoting relaxation and healing), but it was just for my own interest. I couldn't see how I could make a career out of any of them, so I resigned myself to being stuck in an office for ever: chained to my emails, staying small and hidden. There was nothing else out there for me, or so I believed. I shut down my imagination, blocked out my curiosity and turned away

LifeTonic

from my calling. I couldn't see another path because I didn't know what it looked like.

Until it found me.

Sitting at my desk one day, I suddenly heard a voice pipe out: "Quit your job!" Confused, I looked around the office to see who was speaking. No one looked up. The voice spoke again: "Quit your job." Again, I glanced around, and saw no one. Was it a joke? Was someone having a laugh at my expense? A few minutes passed and I carried on working. Once again, the voice piped up. So I got up, and went into the toilet where I sat down and closed my eyes. I took some deep breaths and began to chat to the voice: "OK, I can hear you. If this means I'm mad, at least no one's here to witness it. Why are you telling me to quit my job? Is there a plan B? A nicer, better-paid job I can walk into?"

There was complete silence, so I kept speaking: "I'll do what you say, but my partner and I are about to buy a flat, so I need to know that I'll be supported! Are you listening? Do you hear me? I need some reassurance, or a sign that you have my back." After a few more seconds, a word dropped quietly and calmly into my mind: "Trust." And that was that.

I realised then that the voice had been speaking from inside of me. It wasn't someone in the office; it was my inner GPS (or my intuition), which was guiding me in the most obvious way possible. It felt safe and reassuring, a trusted voice – like Sir David Attenborough's. So I didn't question it. I knew exactly what I needed to do.

Before I had a chance to chicken out, I waltzed right up to my boss and asked him for five minutes. It was as if a supernatural force took over my mind and tongue, and spoke on my behalf. I calmly explained that I didn't really know why I wanted to leave, but that it just felt right to do so. I referenced the couple of mistakes that had happened recently (not entirely my fault, but I was probably self-sabotaging without realising it). I'm sure he was surprised but he accepted my resignation gracefully. What other choice did he have?

I remember how light I felt. I could smell the freedom and taste the possibilities. On paper it wasn't the best timing as I'd be out of work for a while, but I wasn't freaking out. It felt so right that I was calm. Somehow the not knowing made it all the more exciting! I left work that night with a new spring in my step, and the world at my feet. Things were opening up. I couldn't see what was next but I didn't need to. I'd been told to trust and so I did. My hairs were standing on end, and my cheeks flushed with excitement for the first time in a long while.

Setting up my business

Let's be completely clear, I had nothing to go to, nada! No plan, no goals, no direction. I was totally and utterly clueless about what to do next. But I didn't panic. I did what the voice asked me to do. I'd been set free and so I went on holiday and recovered. While away I created my first DIY website, offering my services as a healer, and that made me think about what I wanted to do and how I wanted to feel doing it.

I dreamed of finding my own thing, something I'd love doing even during the tough times. I wanted to jump out of bed each morning full of energy and passion, and feel forever grateful that I had left my old career.

My intuition was telling me to look further afield and find people who were making a success out of healing businesses. In the US, I found some stories that sounded similar to mine. This gave me hope, and I began to envision myself as a "brand".

Around the same time, I read a book about "free-ranging" (for details, see page 260). This basically means escaping the nine to five, creating a life you love and still paying the bills, which made a lot of sense to me. I realised I wasn't alone, that my entrepreneurial spirit would keep me going, and I wouldn't fail. I was a hard worker, with tons of business experience and I knew it would always be possible to make a living. I knew that I wouldn't be homeless – a deep fear that most of us hold without realising it. So now, not only did I believe I'd be OK, I began to realise I could do something incredible. I just had to be patient enough to wait and find out what that "something" was.

Trusting in the universe

The problem with listening to the voices in your head is that there will be negative, critical ones to throw you off course, as well as the divine and positive ones who have your back. The negative ones sound worried, full of fear, shout to get your attention and give you commands. The divine ones sound loving, reassuring and they speak more softly. We mostly hear the fear and get stuck because we can't see the next step. Whenever we're unable to see what's ahead, we panic and slam on the brakes.

In my case I heard streams of endless chatter in my head: "You're not ready to share this with the world."; "That's not funny enough to post on Instagram."; "It's too scary to get on stage and talk about that. What if no one likes what you have to say?" or (my personal favourite): "If you ask them for support, they might think you're desperate."

When you think about taking a leap into the unknown, there will be lots of people around you telling you not to do it.

These might be the voices of your parents, teachers, friends or siblings saying that you shouldn't take financial risks, that you should "never, ever go into business for yourself", that you are "not good enough", that it will be "too scary". It can take courage to disregard them and stick to your path.

Maybe you've had bad experiences in the past when trying to do something similar and this has created a block that stands in the way of you moving forwards now.

Here's some advice I usually give when working with someone who feels blocked:

- ◆ **It's likely you won't know where the next step is.** Get used to this idea. The brave bit is taking a big leap of faith, and allowing the universe to catch up with you – which it will.

- **Trust that inner voice guiding you to jump ship, and open up to other possibilities.** You're being guided because it's the right time, and because there's something else waiting for you. In opening up first, you'll begin to say to the universe, "Yes, I'm ready for the next thing", and hopefully something else will begin to open up for you.

- **It's totally possible to earn a living from doing anything you're passionate about.** Period. The hardest part is usually finding that thing. But it will find you; it might have already.

- **Whenever we're grateful for something, we raise our spirits or our "vibration", and this helps us attract more good things into our lives.** Be grateful for everything during any time of transition: the fridge full of food, the birds singing in the trees, the roses in the park and so on.

- **It's OK not to have all the answers.** They'll come as you keep going forwards. Oh how I wish someone had told me that.

- **Be alert for any signs that appear.** Maybe there's a new documentary about the exact subject you're interested in. Perhaps you meet someone who works with some useful contacts. An ad that pops up on Facebook might provide your next step. Keep your eyes and your heart open for signs from the universe.

> **How are you going to release your blocks? Take out your LifeTonic notebook and answer all those critical voices.**
>
> ◆ Why is this idea the right thing for you?
>
> ◆ Why are you not going to let the negative voices win?
>
> ◆ Explain how this challenge will help your process of healing.
>
> ◆ What will you gain from following your passion?

My business was born from an open heart and a willingness to trust in the universe.

I had no fixed ideas, except an inner knowing that it would be something magical, and this was all I needed. Each time I tuned into the energy of what I'd be creating, my hairs would stand on end and butterflies would flutter in my tummy. I simply walked blindly on, half-hoping, half-knowing I was making the right decision.

Releasing my self-imposed blocks allowed energy to flow through me. It's easier to create amazing things without any limitations in the way. Imagine that your new thing is an expression of you, and prepare to pour your effort, time, focus, concentration, thoughts, feelings, emotions and love (all these things are energy) into it.

Imagine all you could achieve if those negative voices didn't stand in your way. Your potential would be limitless. You'd be successful beyond measure. You'd be unstoppable. And that's why it's crucial to invest in yourself and heal. It's a commitment, and it's the only way to silence the inner voices.

Everyone's a teacher

I have many teachers: people I meet who have amazing wisdom to share and new things to teach me. Sometimes it's a fleeting exchange, and sometimes it's a conversation that continues for a lifetime. Whether they know it or not, they're teaching me something profound about myself and my life: my relationships, my career, my health (and the rest). They're always a gift to me in some way.

I believe everyone I come into contact with is teaching me something. I've found that if you adopt this belief, it'll help you be more open to receiving more lessons.

Some of my most obvious teachers are:

- **my clients,** who teach me something about myself in every single session;
- **my groups of clients,** who teach me about a hundred things in one sitting;
- **my friends,** who are always teaching me new things about myself, and guiding me through my life;
- **my partner,** who is the biggest teacher of all;

- **my entire family,** who are all great teachers – they have known me my whole life, and they know how to push my buttons!

These people are constantly teaching me things without necessarily being aware of it. Sometimes it takes me a while to receive the lesson, so they keep reminding me over and over again. When the same things keep happening, or the same patterns are on repeat, it's usually because I haven't quite completed my "homework".

Actually, there are people waiting to teach you things on every street corner, and they don't even know it – neither do you. When I say "teach", often they trigger you and open something up deep inside you. It could be an old woman at a bus stop who says something profound. It could be a delivery man or someone who comes to read the electricity meter. Whether this makes sense to you or not, remain open to the possibility because your life will start to open up in a new way if you do.

When I learned this whole "everybody's-teaching-you-some-thing" concept, it took a long time to sink in. Perhaps it's hard to admit when we're adults that we're actually still learning something new all the time. Maybe we feel we should already know it?

And what I've found is that most of the time, whatever these teachers are trying to teach us involves areas we haven't been able to look at yet. Simply being open to this idea suddenly makes things much easier and the lessons will pour in. Then you can transform, and life makes more sense. "Woo-hoo! Sign me up," I hear you say.

Finding your way in times of change

Whenever we sense change coming, our instinct is to cling on and stay where we are. Change is scary. When the pressure is on to find something else, it's easy to get lost in the fear. We want immediate certainty and look outside for answers, but they aren't there because the answers we need are inside. When we worry, we contract and close down, and then we might miss the universal signs guiding us to what's next.

Here are some things you can do to help yourself find your own path:

+ **Trust.** When you find the path that's right for you, the universe will support you in pursuing it. Some people find it helpful to introduce a mantra (a positive phrase which you repeat often, either out loud or in your head). It could be: "I trust in the universe, I trust I'll be supported and I surrender and let go of fear."

+ **Continue to work on healing yourself.** Do all the Tonics as you work through this book but if you feel you need extra support, look for a healer, coach or alternative practitioner who will help you release your blocks.

+ **Meditation is an incredibly helpful tool.** I'll be talking more about it later in the book. When we quiet the mind chatter and slow everything down, we can hear our own inner wisdom coming from deep inside.

- **Picture your new life.** Create a vision board where you stick inspiring images to help you create the sense of how you want to feel when you're doing what you love. This is what you want your life to be like. This is where you are heading for – starting now.

People Pleasing

I care about what people think of me, I really do. I care too much, and I wish I didn't.

I'm sure you can relate to this. On the whole, we are a nation of people pleasers, programmed to be polite, form orderly queues and apologise even when we're not in the wrong.

As a fairly consistent people pleaser for the majority of my life, I've done and said lots of things I didn't want to, purely to please others. And it's only now I'm coming to recognise how much of an impact this has had on my life, and the way it's affected my sense of identity.

I'm not suggesting that we shouldn't do things for friends and work colleagues, or go out of our way to help loved ones when they need us, but if you continually sacrifice your own happiness for the sake of others in an attempt to "earn" their friendship or love, then you're pushing your own needs to the bottom of the list and there will be side effects. Trust me, I'm an expert in this and I've learned the hard way.

The negative effects of people pleasing

Imagine how a best friend or lover would feel if you repeatedly ignored them and their needs, and focused all your time and energy on other people instead. Let down and rejected? Unappreciated and disrespected by you? And rightly so! They'd probably walk away and leave you to it. Why should they stick around when all you do is ignore them and don't respect their needs? It would take some major recognition and heart-felt apologies from you to make things right. Plus some solid time and investment in the relationship.

It's exactly the same with yourself. When you're constantly pleasing other people, you are that best friend or lover who is being ignored – except you can't walk away. When you ignore yourself, it hurts you deep inside. You feel rejected and let down, which affects your mood and state of mind. You definitely won't feel very happy or respected. When this is how you're feeling on the inside, it will show on the outside too and you'll attract situations that make you feel even more rejected and let down because that's the way life works!

And not only does it affect you, it also affects the people you are pleasing.

When you're doing things simply to please others, they can sense that you're not being your authentic self, and on some level it makes them uncomfortable.

Think about it. We all have that friend who says "yes" to everything and then cancels at the last minute because she's treble-booked herself. (Yet all too often it turns out she's known she couldn't meet you on that day for the last month or so.) She never seems to mind what you do when you're together; she is super-eager to make you happy and goes along with everyone else's plans. She never seems to have an opinion and agrees with what you say most of the time. She doesn't appear to know her own mind. And if you're anything like me, it annoys you. Perhaps it just annoys me because it reminds me of me! Now that I'm aware of this trait in myself, it makes me cringe when I see it in others.

The nature of people pleasing – to hold yourself back and put others first – can be detrimental to your progression in life. For example, in your career or business it can create lots of procrastination. You can't possibly please everyone – men, women, mothers, teenagers, spiritual people, non-spiritual people, etc. – when they all have very different needs. When I first planned my business I was trying to be all things to all people, and I tripped over myself in the confusion. Rather than moving forwards quickly with an amazing idea, or some brilliant wisdom or an inspiring post, people pleasers fiddle until it's totally perfect and the message gets diluted.

Think about how it can impact your voice on social media, for example. If your main goal is to be "liked" or get the most amount of "likes" possible, you won't be focusing on the quality and honesty of your message. If you're trying to please lots of people with the "right" message, it won't feel or sound authentic and people won't like it anyway. It's much better to bite the bullet and start putting yourself out there in your own way. You'll get so much more respect when you do.

It all comes down to this: being yourself first and foremost, so that when you do something for someone else you do it because you want to, because you care for them. They will know this and appreciate it, and your words and actions will carry authentic love and give more impact. It's a win-win situation, and you'll feel great in the process!

Unpicking learned behaviours

All this is much easier said than done. I know, because it's something I've personally struggled with for years. I've been slowly but surely unpicking the layers, and unravelling the pleasing behaviours I learned as a child.

If you're a people pleaser like me, at some point down the line you decided that it was the best way to move through your life. Perhaps you saw your parents do it, and you learned by mirroring them. Perhaps they weren't around all that much when you were a child and so when they were there, you'd do everything you could to be "good" to ensure you received the most praise and attention possible. Maybe one of your parents left, and now you want to make doubly sure that none of your friends or partners walk away or reject you, because you don't want to feel that pain again.

Once you understand why you have a tendency to people please, you'll find you have a greater compassion and understanding for yourself. You were trying your best to avoid being ignored, rejected and abandoned but really all you want is to be loved, seen, and accepted. And this is something you can work on. It's a big part of what this book is about.

I still struggle with people pleasing to this day, partly because I don't like to let anyone down. All my old childhood insecurities come to the surface when I'm around people who are confident, bold, opinionated and confrontational. It's heightened by the fact that I've given up drinking alcohol in social situations, so I don't have that crutch to lean on any more. It's the real me, wounds and all, without the help of Prosecco; I feel exposed and vulnerable and I'm not completely comfortable with being 100 per cent "me". I'm very sensitive to other people's energy in these situations, and can pick up on even the slightest negative vibe or pull-back. As soon as I feel someone pulling away, I go into über-people-pleasing mode and try even harder to make them like me.

When I started working with private clients, offering intuitive healing sessions, I had big lessons to learn about boundaries. Without even being conscious of it, I was inviting them to enter into my personal space and giving way more time in a session than they had paid for. Sometimes I'd be on the phone to clients outside of work hours, or receiving long emails asking for lots of my energy and focus. After a while I realised I'd get more respect, and my sessions would be more effective if I learned how to be firm and worry less about feeling that I'd let clients down. As soon as I began to stick to clearer boundaries and professional terms and conditions, my clients responded positively. I would give them all the healing available to them within our session, but any other problems had to be saved up for the next paid-for time. Being clear on this works for everyone.

I'm still working on clearer boundaries in the right place when it comes to social contacts, friends and family, because there are no contracts, no rules. I want to give out to the people I love, but only so long as I am still being true to myself.

The main way to overcome your people-pleasing behaviours is to create a deeper relationship with yourself.

It's something we will be looking at in more detail in the second half of this book. When you're pleasing people, you're seeking external validation that what you're doing is right. When you do this, your success can then become dependent on how well-liked you are by others. Instead, you need to find an internal validation from yourself, to create a loving relationship with yourself and feel loved from the inside out. When you do, you won't need external validation; you'll already know how much you rock!

The second thing I'm understanding more about now is that it's OK for some people not to like you. Certain people will never like you, or what you stand for. It's probably because they have their own issues going on; maybe you trigger some of their deep-seated childhood anxieties or they don't respect your values. This is something we all have to learn to accept. People might not like you, and that is OK. There are certain people you won't like either, so it works both ways.

> **Write in your LifeTonic notebook about your own experiences of people pleasing.**
>
> ◆ Can you think of anything you've done for someone else and then resented? Why did you do it? What did you worry would happen if you didn't? Would you do it again if they asked now?
>
> ◆ Are there some people in your friendship group or family who always make you feel guilty if you don't help them out?
>
> ◆ Are there any people pleasers in your immediate circle? How do they make you feel?

Give and take

The message of this chapter is not that you should stop doing anything for anyone else – far from it! I believe you should always be as loving to others as you possibly can. The more positive energy you put out into the universe, the more you will get back. This means little things like giving a big smile and saying "have a great day" to the person in the coffee shop who hands you your latte; and bigger things like giving up your time to visit a sick, elderly relative, or child-minding for a friend while she goes for a job interview.

In close relationships, I advocate giving loads of love – so long as it's truly meant at the time. Authentic, specific compliments, such as "I really like that colour on you; you're so good at putting outfits together" are a world of difference from a quick "You look great, lovely". A spontaneous, lengthy hug while your partner is cooking dinner will mean much more than the usual quick peck on the lips when you get home from work.

The difference between this and people pleasing is that you're doing it for the right reasons. It comes from a place of inner strength. Love makes the world go round but the first thing to learn is how to be as loving as you can to yourself.

PAUSE AND REFLECT

Wow! You're good. Well done for keeping up. So far, so good.

If you are still with me, you're doing really well and I honour your courage.

As we enter the chill-out zone, it's time to check in with yourself. Take stock of how you're feeling in this very moment. Let's move into a new head/heart space, so you're even more open to receiving healing and wisdom.

- How are you feeling at this moment? I hope you are excited and inspired by what you've learned so far.
- What are you thinking about?
- What planet are you on? Earth or somewhere else?
- What reactions are you having to the book?
- How much resistance are you feeling?

Resistance is a slippery sucker. I mention it often because it's good at disguising itself and a lot of the time you won't even realise it's around. Until you're stuck and procrastinating. That's the resistance I'm talking about. It stops you from thriving in life, so be aware.

You need time to pause. To integrate all that's been learned so far. Our modern problem is the simple lack of time and space to pause and reflect.

Right here is the gift of time and space.

There is more power waiting in the wings for you now, along with a dazzling light to shine brightly out into your world. Be open to the possibility of this. Right now, you are preparing to open up for expansion. You have the power to change your world, and I rejoice in your potential. You have an exciting life ahead, unlimited potential and millions of miracles.

————

"Somewhere inside all of us is the power to change the world."
– Roald Dahl

————

Let's keep going, because together we're stronger, braver, smarter. Continue with me and let's dive into the Tonics, with their powerful Tools and techniques designed to support you in your modern life.

Keep going. It's so worth it. I'm with you every step of the way.

PART TWO

The Tonics

CHAPTER

9

The Toolbox of Tonics

Welcome to your toolbox for surviving modern life! Chapters 10 to 33 in this book will offer you a range of simple "Tools" to heal your modern woes and soothe your soul. When your outside world feels upside down, they will help you understand why. This chapter explains what you'll need to make the most of the Tools.

The time has come to experience some big life changes. You ready?

You might already have noticed your mood changing. Are you feeling more emotional than usual? A little snappier or a bit off-balance? This is because you're preparing for change, and you can sense what's ahead. Your intuitive radar is tuned in, and you know change is coming. Think about the way cows sense rain coming and lie down in the field to prepare. You sense healing and transformation, and so you prepare by clearing space and beginning your clear-out ahead of time.

It's like a mini inner detox to prepare you for the main event.

This is deeper healing. We're about to go deep underground and enter a healing process.

Everyone will start at a different level:

- Some of you will be complete newbies.
- Some of you might dabble in meditation.
- Some of you might go on yoga retreats.
- Some of you might see an acupuncturist, life coach or other type of therapist.

Whichever you align with, there's something here for you. I've been on this journey for six years, and I learn something new every single day. Be open to new possibilities, and you'll go far. Close down and you'll miss out.

Working through the Tonics

In reading this book, you've made the conscious decision to incorporate self-help into your life. You are taking responsibility for your mental, emotional, physical and spiritual health. As you move through the toolbox, you'll feel empowered to take action, and unravel and shed the layers that have been hiding the real you. This is your path to freedom and authentic happiness.

We will begin by creating the foundations of your self-help practice, and then work through a selection of common topics or issues people struggle with.

———

The areas that cause the most resistance and self-sabotage are your greatest opportunities for growth.

———

Most of these you'll easily relate to, and you will understand straight away how they apply to you. Certain topics you might find more difficult to connect to because you're in denial about them. Be alert if you suddenly find you want to skip a chapter and flick through to the next one. Other activities will suddenly seem very important – making a phone call or cleaning the house, for example. This distraction or self-sabotage comes from resistance and is a clear sign that you have unresolved issues with the topic covered in that chapter. Resistance crops up because you're avoiding facing up to old wounds, but unless you persevere, it will block you from receiving the healing you need and making progress with that area of your life.

This happens all the time in our lives. The trick is to become aware of the areas that cause the most resistance and self-sabotage, as they are your greatest opportunities for growth. Face them, and you will make the breakthroughs.

If a topic doesn't apply to you at the moment, it's likely it will at some future stage. Before you turn the page and move on, ask yourself, "How do I feel about this topic?"

Relaxed and neutral?

Tense and tight?

Be honest. If you feel tense, come back to it later.

This is perfect timing

These Tools are my interpretations of teachings I've received from mentors, during meditation, and from my experience with the thousands of individual clients and groups I've had the pleasure of working with.

You might have already received some wisdom from other teachers. I believe that we receive the perfect information at the perfect time for us.

You're reading this book now because it's the perfect time to receive its teachings. Your intuition has guided you here. You'll learn new Tools and be given new information that you can combine with everything you know already. It might form the foundation of your healing knowledge, which you can use to create your own healing system to support you in life.

Here are my nine juiciest life lessons to keep in your back pocket as you work through the Tonics:

1. DETOXING YOUR INSIDES. You are about to experience a clear-out of old emotions and old memories, so feeling some old pain is normal. Imagine a spring-clean of old clothes, old shoes, old accessories and old products you've been hanging onto. Remember how great you feel when you've finished? Lighter, clearer, more organised, calmer and energised. Clearing out of any sort is good for the soul.

2. RELEASING YOUR ENERGY. You may experience yawning, crying, burping or even breaking wind(!) while you're working through the Tonics. This is energy moving through you, working its way out and being released. We're full of energy, so we release it during any process of transition. I often burp while the energy moves through me and I like to think of it as my spiritual champagne! Do you often cry?

Crying is another form of release that should leave you feeling relieved afterwards.

3. ASK FOR SUPPORT. When anything feels too overwhelming, and too much to handle, you must ask for support. You're now responsible for your own wellbeing, so you have to learn how to take care of yourself. This means knowing when you need support, and reaching out. You'll be better able to support yourself long-term if you seek the extra support when you need it.

4. BUILD UP YOUR TOOLBOX. As you go through each Tonic, learn the points and Tools. Even if the topic doesn't resonate at this very moment, it will do at some stage; if not for you, then perhaps for your child, your partner or parent. It's worth knowing the Tools, so you have the wisdom to hand should you need it.

5. NOTHING IS WASTED. Every single thing you learn will be important to you in some way. Even if you think you don't need the information now, everything you absorb will be useful in later life. Taking time to understand the topics and learn the knowledge will mean that life brings you even more experiences. You now understand how to deal with difficult situations you might not have handled well before.

6. BE CURIOUS. When we approach topics with a curious mind or heart, we're much more open to whatever happens. Curiosity creates opening, and allows you to receive life in a richer way. Be curious about the feelings or thoughts that emerge from your inner self as you move through the process.

7. BELIEVE IN MAGIC. Be open to all possibilities. It's easy to brush something off because you can't see it with the naked eye. The more open you are to believing in the impossible, the unachievable or the unavailable, the more the magic will happen.

8. HONOUR YOUR FEELINGS. Invite your feelings to be here with you. It's normal to feel emotions coming up to the surface, negative or positive. It's important to support yourself through all processes, and stay calm with whatever you feel. Remember: you're having an inner detox, you're clearing out the old to make space for the new.

9. RESISTANCE IS GREAT. This is so important, I'm telling you twice! The topics you feel the most resistance to are your biggest opportunities for growth. This is life's best-kept secret. Once you are aware that resistance is hiding something juicy, you'll learn how to work through it and receive what's on the other side. Watch out for the topics you most want to run away from and keep them on your list of priorities, because these are pure gold.

———

"Those who don't believe in magic will never find it."
– Roald Dahl

———

How to work through the Tonics

Work through the Tonics at your own pace. This is a marathon, not a sprint. If you're on holiday, you could work through them all in a fortnight, but if you're at home and life is busy, perhaps focus on one Tonic per week.

You can work through the Tonics in the order they are printed, or pick and choose according to your mood. But be mindful of the areas you're keen to skip past, because these will provide the juiciest healing!

Each time you repeat a Tonic, you'll work deeper with it, and more insight will rise to the surface.

I have produced some extra audio content to accompany you on your *LifeTonic* journey. This includes guided meditations and other Tonics to support and supplement your experience. You'll find information on how to access it on my website www.jodyshield.co.uk

Before you start with the Tonics, you will need:

- **A notebook and pen.** Lots of what you'll learn will sink in without you making notes, but it's good to write down new discoveries and information that rise to the surface as you work your way through. Treat yourself to a nice new notebook and pen if you didn't invest earlier.

- **Tissues.** Just sayin' . . . this is emotional work, so it's likely you'll need tissues. Crying is good for the soul, as you are releasing old emotional energy.

- **A mirror**. This is a great tool for self-encouragement. Speaking to yourself in the mirror takes practice, and it will feel unnatural or uncomfortable at first, but the mirror is one of the most powerful Tools of transformation. I use it all the time.

- **Water**. Stay hydrated, flush out your toxins and get cleansed.

- **A sacred space**. I'll tell you about this in the next chapter.

Before we go any further, I need to know that you're in this with me. Are you really and truly in with both feet?

Take a moment to assess your status right now. Are you being cautious, and thinking you'll just dip your toe in? Are you trusting a little bit more and willing to be half in? Or are you ready to be fully immersed in this with me?

There are no judgements, whichever you choose. Just accept where you're at, so we can clear any weeds or sabotage out of the way. But if you're fully in, or at least willing to be fully in, you'll shift much faster.

Do you want to shift your stuff? Do you want to feel clearer, more positive and happy about life again?

Great! In that case, let's jump right in!

Oh, and if you're feeling a tad uncomfortable, that's a good thing! From personal experience, you never truly learn anything unless you're feeling uncomfortable in some way.

And we're off . . .

CHAPTER

10

Design Your Sacred Space

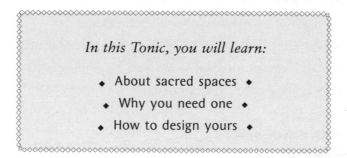

In this Tonic, you will learn:

♦ About sacred spaces ♦
♦ Why you need one ♦
♦ How to design yours ♦

You need a home within your home. A den. A divine cave. A sacred space just for you.

Somewhere to express yourself, however you choose.

A space full of magical possibilities, where new life is created before your very eyes.

You'll feel alive in this place: your very own celestial spot buzzing with creative energy and cosmic possibilities.

This is your territory. It's a place within your home, with the essence of "you" inside it. It's a container of your divine energy, an area where you've made your mark. It can be a cosy corner in the bedroom, a snuggly space in the spare room or a beautiful spot in your home office. Somewhere big enough for a small table to hold your objects. You're going to cover this table and the surrounding area with things that lift your energy and brighten your inner light.

There could be more than one location: you might have a specific space for your practice and healing processes, and other environments that inspire you when you need a boost. For me, these include: my cosy office, which is full of creative inspiration, and my beautiful bed. Not only do I sleep there, but it's also a place for meditation in the morning and the evening. I have a big, fluffy cushion propped behind me.

You're going to design your very own blissful space (or spaces) with the purpose of healing and aiding spiritual practice. It's a place of cosmic affairs!

A sanctuary of peace

At times, life can be rocky and unpredictable. It slaps us in the face when we're least expecting it. Even in the most positive rays of sunshine, we can still feel dark clouds of anger and frustration moving through us. Life can be overwhelming when it throws up all kinds of dirty laundry, which spills over into our relationships and our work. We'll be set tests, and forced to make tough decisions. We'll be dredging up heavy emotions and, of course, pain. None of us is immune to this, yet some are better equipped to deal with it than others, as we have more Tools. After reading this book, you'll have a whole toolbox to support you to cope with life.

When life bashes us about, it's easy to spiral out of control and into negative headspace; this is the default response. It can be tough to pull ourselves out again when we have sunk into deep negativity. To counteract this, we need somewhere to step into where we can reset; a place of inspiration where we immediately feel uplifted.

When we're on a self-help or spiritual journey, we're constantly healing and expanding. We need somewhere to anchor ourselves down, so we can feel safe to transform. Our sacred space becomes a destination for transformation, and holds the energy of change supporting us to do so more.

Filling your sacred space

Select a comfy chair or cushion to sit on, and gather together your most sacred treasures. Fill your space with items that inspire and excite you, that invoke magical memories, and raise you up. Find goods that you treasure, objects from faraway lands, things that other people might tell you are "clutter". These are personal to you, so it doesn't matter what they think.

My space contains:

◆ an antique table with a pearlised design in a hexagon shape;
◆ two big crystals: a pink rose quartz and a big cluster of clear quartz;
◆ a jade buddha on a wooden stand from a faraway land, which belonged to my granny;
◆ natural scented candles; I love watching the flames;
◆ a crystal in the shape of a pestle which is green and pink for creative flow;

- worded affirmations on paper from my Light Grids teacher, Damien Wynne;
- roses — sometimes fake and sometimes real;
- a dreamcatcher my boyfriend gave me at the festival where we met;
- some special stones given to me by friends;
- colour essences that smell divine;
- tapestries from an indigenous tribe in the Amazon;
- incense;
- a meditation cushion to sit on;
- a sheepskin fur rug.

All these things make me feel instantly uplifted and happy. Now it's your turn.

Tools to create your own sacred space:

1. **LOCATION SCOUTING.** Go on a hunt around your house, scouting for the perfect place. You might find a couple of different spaces, so assess the practicalities of each and decide on the best one. You can always try out a couple until you figure out what works best for you.

2. **COLLECT YOUR TREASURE.** Select a table that fits in your space, and think of possessions you can place on it that lift you up. Once you start thinking about finding your treasures, a strange thing will happen and they will find you.

3. SELECT THE RIGHT SEAT. Buy a chair or cushion that feels supportive and comfortable. A meditation cushion can be transformational for your practice.

4. SHOP FOR NEW TREASURE. This is the exciting part: treat yourself to some new treasure. If crystals are your thing, head over to your favourite shop. You'll also find some lovely ones on the shop section on my website.

5. NOURISH YOUR SACRED SPACE. Go there often and add to the space. If things feel out of place or old, replace them. Prune back the weeds and plant new seeds. Think of it as an ever-evolving space. Add in nature through houseplants and fresh flowers.

———

Your sacred space is for introspection, contemplation, meditation, self-examination. It's for stillness, reflection, creation and "you" time.

———

Make it transcendent. Make it cosy and personal to you. Savour your space and flourish within it.

11

Meditate not Medicate

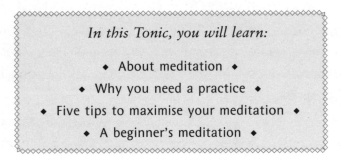

In this Tonic, you will learn:

◆ About meditation ◆

◆ Why you need a practice ◆

◆ Five tips to maximise your meditation ◆

◆ A beginner's meditation ◆

There's no right or wrong way to meditate. There's **your** way, and that's the best way. It's a practice, so it's something you get better at the more you do it. Telling ourselves we're not doing it right or we're not good enough at meditating is a common barrier. And we don't need any more excuses. It's hard enough to maintain a practice, especially one that's positive and nourishing for us.

Meditation offers a connection to your higher self/higher wisdom/higher intelligence/intuition (use whatever word makes sense to you) with many other benefits. This higher self aspect is easier to access once the mind is quiet and you're relaxed and calm. The benefit of accessing this part of you is that it helps you to understand more about yourself on a deeper level: what lights you up, how you can thrive, how you raise your vibes.

Meditation is also about surrendering: releasing control, relaxing your body and mind and letting go of resistance. We cling on tightly to life, pushing events forwards, forcing things to happen. This creates tension inside us, and over time it stacks up. As adults we're full of tension, and we're not taught how to release it. This is one of our main struggles in life.

There are many types of meditation, including mindfulness, visualisation and Transcendental, or TM. Every technique offers a different perspective, but they all have a similar goal: to quieten the mind. You can then more easily hear your inner voice or intuition coming from your higher self. If you already meditate using a certain technique, keep practising but be open to incorporating some new teachings. It's good to have variation.

The many benefits of meditation

A big part of meditation involves training the mind to slow down, so the thoughts get quieter. This is sometimes achieved by giving your mind something else to focus on, such as your breathing or a certain point in your body.

When your inner world slows down, your outer world does too and you become more present. One of the benefits is that you become more productive. Sound counterintuitive?

We've learned to work harder and faster to achieve great things, but when you meditate, your mind becomes clearer, quieter and there's more space for new creative solutions.

This means less time wasted, more focus and faster problem-solving.

There are many scientifically proven benefits of meditation, including:

- reduced reactivity of the amygdala: the fight-or-flight-response part of the brain usually operates in overdrive, but meditation calms it down and reduces the dangerous side effects of chronic stress on the body;
- increased activity in the prefrontal cortex: this helps to regulate the emotions and reduce stress;
- improved divergent thinking: a style of thinking that encourages creativity and new ideas;
- increased compassion: alters the parts of the brain responsible for empathy;
- increased focus: concentration is sharpened;
- managing anxiety: the parts of the brain responsible for regulating thoughts about yourself are altered.

"How to meditate" was the fourth most-searched question powered by Google in 2014, so clearly we want to know how to do it. Our friends are talking about it, our GPs are recommending it for combatting stress and we've read articles suggesting it's the best-kept secret of the world's most successful CEOs.

Meditation is needed more than ever before to counteract the increasing amount of stress and anxiety in our workaholic society. Fortunately it's more readily available than ever before with online classes, YouTube videos and many workplaces offering wellbeing sessions.

Meditation has been the single most important thing for me and has changed my life completely since I started in 2010 in Peru. It's elevated my enthusiasm, my focus, my passion for what I do, and given me the Tools to live a more compassionate life. And most of all, it's increased my energy, a huge shift for me as I was always tired and drained.

Still need more reasons to practise meditation?

- **Meditation helps you clear out the past.** You hold onto unresolved past experiences, and wait for the right time to process and release them. Meditation offers that space. Have some tissues ready.

- **Meditation helps you to sleep well.** A client once told me that my meditation session had cured her of a lifetime of insomnia. Sleep is vital to living a healthy, happy life.

- **Meditation helps you reset.** The rest you receive in deep meditation is scientifically proven to be deeper than sleep. Your energy levels will soar, and you'll move into a new phase of the day when you emerge.

- **Meditation is vital for transformation.** Whenever you're working on healing yourself, it's important you allocate time to meditate, and tune into you. Create the space to receive new wisdom and insight about you and your progress.

- **Meditation teaches you how to receive.** Whether you realise it or not, when you meditate you connect to your higher self. You receive information and energy during the experience. You learn to surrender when receiving the meditation, as opposed to trying to control it – a common confusion in meditation practice.

Overcoming resistance

Meditation is a practice. It needs to be participated in regularly. In our quick-fix society, we've lost understanding of the word "practice", and the effort needed when learning something new. It's easy to find excuses to not do something. Resistance and procrastination will increase as time goes on; they always do when we're trying anything beneficial for our personal growth.

Ask yourself: how committed am I to changing my life? If the answer is "very" or, at the very least, "I'm open to it" or "I'm willing to", that's enough to begin a change. And to those of you who are not very good at practising, it'll be because of your resistance getting in the way and sabotaging your progress. If you become more aware of your resistance, you can work with it; just invite it to be here, and you will become better.

When you're starting anything new, it's easy to feel overwhelmed and believe you're not doing it right. Especially with meditation. I've spoken to people who've been to one class and then decided they can't do it because it's too hard to focus. Hello? Meditation is a practice; no one's perfect at first.

A meditation practice is like making your bed in the morning. You know you should do it as it'll kick-start your day, organise your mind, and make you feel well and happy, but you wake up late, dash into the shower and forget. You do this on repeat. Your bed remains messy, and you feel dirty when you climb into the crumpled sheets at bedtime.

If I said to you that you only needed to meditate for ten minutes a day to notice a big difference, would you believe me? Ten minutes is shorter than an average daily shower. Isn't it worth a try?

If by this point you're still asking "Why should I do it?" then I ask you to take my word for it for now. Meditation is life-changing when you commit to it. If I ever get asked "What is the number-one thing you can do to ensure your transformation?" I'd always give the answer "Meditation" without even hesitating!

Learn how to meditate – a beginner's guide:

1. Go to your sacred space (see Chapter 10) or any other quiet place where you won't be disturbed. It's ideal if you have a meditation cushion but a comfy chair will also do. Sit down but don't lie down, which might make you fall asleep.

2. Close your eyes and place your hand over the centre of your chest – your "energetic heart centre".

3. Take a nice, deep breath into your chest and observe how the hand rises and space is created inside you. As you breathe out, notice how the hand falls and your body folds and softens.

4. Keep breathing in and out, and get used to connecting your breath to your hand over your heart's centre and the feeling of your chest rising and falling.

5. Rather than controlling your breath, imagine yourself standing back and observing it.

6. Stay like this for a few minutes. As other thoughts come into your head, see them, observe them and notice them but let them pass gently by without engaging with them.

7. Don't judge yourself if you lose focus. Notice when you wander off, and gently move your focus back to your hand over your heart's centre, rising and falling.

8. Do this for ten minutes each morning for a week and notice how you feel in yourself. I guarantee you'll see a difference.

Also try out other guided meditations. There are plenty on the Internet, or go to classes. I have several on my website (see page 260).

Remember that it's a practice: the more you do, the more you'll get out of it.

CHAPTER

12

Moving Inside

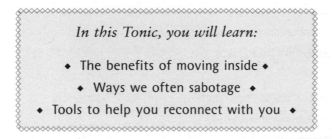

In this Tonic, you will learn:

◆ The benefits of moving inside ◆
◆ Ways we often sabotage ◆
◆ Tools to help you reconnect with you ◆

When you move inside and reconnect with yourself, you become more aware of your own needs. You listen to your own feelings, and act on them. You become more authentic, because you're listening to yourself and expressing your unique messages to your peers. You inspire and motivate other people to listen to themselves as well.

—————

Listening to yourself means listening to your heart, and your inner guidance or intuition.

—————

This gives you information about where you're heading, and how to get there in the best way for you.

You become more aware of how you're living your life. Usually we're just going through the motions, something that more spiritually aware people might refer to as "asleep". Of course, you're really awake, but it means you're closed down to the wider possibilities and disconnected from yourself.

Moving inside and reconnecting with yourself is a practice. It's something you have to keep doing before you learn how to trust yourself, hear yourself and be fully present in your life. Practise this reconnection, and you'll transform faster than you ever thought possible.

The benefits of connecting

Usually when advice is needed, we ask others (Google, our friends, partner or family) and then listen to the answers. Our information comes from the outside world, and is filtered through our minds and our belief systems. If the information doesn't make sense, we'll decide whether to process or discard it. When someone else gives us advice, it's through their filters and their belief systems, which are based on their past experiences. So why don't we ask ourselves for advice?

We've become very good at not listening to our inner voice. We lack trust in ourselves because we've all been hurt in the past after making a wrong decision. We're not sure how to ask our inner voice for advice, and we don't know how to hear the reply. This isn't surprising, because we're much more connected to our "mind's voice".

Our mind's voice and our inner voice are not the same thing. One is the voice of your thoughts (thinking), and one is the voice of your intuition (feeling). The voice of your mind is usually loud, bossy and negative, as it's afraid. The voice of your intuition is softer, processed through body sensations and offers calm advice. Over time you can learn to trust the advice of your intuition; follow it and it will speak to you more often.

When you listen to yourself, and act on the wisdom you receive, you'll begin to hear more and more of it. Because you're being guided, you'll feel more confident in your decision-making and less confused about the right path to take. The more confident you feel in your own skin, the better your self-esteem and you will naturally become more productive. You're prioritising your own needs and doing what's best for you, so you'll feel a greater sense of self-love and self-care.

When you're more connected to yourself, it's easier to heal the pains of the past because you sense your blocks and negative patterns. You notice your progress and the way you're changing, which encourages you to keep going.

———

Imagine our intuition coming from a huge
inner library full of wisdom and insight,
which we access through our hearts,
our bodies and our souls.

———

Remembering to connect to ourselves, and listen to our inner voice, is something we all need to re-learn. On a spiritual level, we already know how to do this, because it's part of our blueprint. Imagine the instructions lying dormant in our system, waiting to be activated.

Watch out for self-sabotage

There's so much distraction in life that our minds willingly wander off and find other things to replace anything that involves our self-care or spiritual practice. We walk around with our heads in the clouds, engrossed in our Facebook feeds; we sit on the train, glued to our phones or morning papers. We're so good at distraction that we do it on auto-pilot.

It's easy to self-sabotage when we begin the practice of moving inside and listening to our inner voice. Why? Because when we obtain this unique insight, the guidance it gives invites us to be brighter, bolder and bigger as we follow our spiritual selves. In doing so, we transform and expand, and somewhere deep inside there's a part that wants to stay small and hidden. This part will sabotage progress because it's scared of us being more powerful, more self-confident and more visible in the world. More people will see our "authentic selves" than ever before. We're not hiding behind masks the way we used to. The mere thought of our power and what we might do with it is enough to freak us out.

Is your resistance rising? Invite it to be present – all of it. Remember that resistance shows up when there's an opportunity for a major breakthrough and transformation. Resistance is a positive sign, offering insight and often a huge gift.

Tools to help you move inside and get reconnected to yourself:

1. FOCUS ON YOU. Start asking yourself out loud, "How am I feeling?" on your way to work every morning. Or, even better, ask yourself in the mirror while you're getting ready for work. You will feel uncomfortable when you first face the mirror because you're seeing yourself, with all of your "scars". But the faster you "see" yourself again, the sooner you'll be able to accept what you're seeing.

2. LISTEN TO YOUR BODY. Close your eyes and listen to your body. What can you sense? Listen very carefully. You are looking for very subtle movements, energies moving through, funny twinges or gentle pains. Become used to hearing your body. Does it feel heavy? Does it feel full? Does it feel tight or tense? I am often guided to go to a particular part of my body, maybe my heart or my stomach, and I softly observe what I sense. Don't judge your body; sit with however you feel. You can acknowledge what you're feeling or hearing. The more you become used to connecting with your body in this way, the more it will speak to you.

3. FEEL YOUR HEART. With your eyes closed, place your hand over your heart. The energetic or spiritual heart is right in the centre of your chest, while the physical heart is located towards the left-hand side. Move your hand so the palm rests in the centre of your chest, and the fingers expand downwards over your physical heart. Connect to both places. How does your heart feel? What can you sense? Do you feel the energy moving gently around? Does it feel heavy or blocked or painful? Can you feel the heartbeat? Focus on this for a few moments. This is enough to get you more connected to your heart. This might not be easy at first, but persist and practise. If you feel resistance, simply allow it to be there and sooner or later it will begin to move or melt away.

4. EASIER DECISIONS. At times, making the "right" decisions for you can be tricky. To get clearer try focusing in on the energy of the decision and seeing how your body reacts. Think of a decision you have to make and bring your focus to it. Don't overthink this; just because the decision isn't a physical thing you can see, doesn't mean you can't feel it as energy. If the decision you're tuning into causes your body to expand and open, it's usually an indication of a good decision. If your body contracts or closes, it's a general indication of a not-so-good decision.

Pull Yourself Together

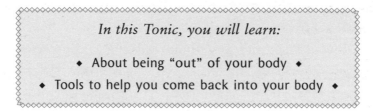

In this Tonic, you will learn:

◆ About being "out" of your body ◆
◆ Tools to help you come back into your body ◆

The practice of "pulling yourself together" forms the foundation of your spiritual development, and will enable you to expand further, because more of your energy and presence will be anchored in your body.

Pulling ourselves back together means we can face the world with more strength and presence. We can also process more of our past and heal at a deeper level.

We're energetically "out" of our bodies. If you could see your energy body overlaid with your physical body, you'd see a proportion in the physical body, and much of it outside the body and fragmented in many different directions. It's the reason we often feel off-balance, wobbly and lost, as if we're floating around aimlessly.

When we're out of our bodies, it's as if our "inner home" has been left unlocked and unguarded, with the doors and windows wide open. Anyone or anything can take up residence.

How we leave our bodies

Emotional trauma of any kind creates a feeling of not being safe in your body, and so without realising it, you energetically and psychologically escape and leave your body. This happens most often in childhood, because you don't want to be present while you experience the pain or negativity. Something as minor as making a mistake while reading out loud in front of your primary-school class can create emotional trauma. You escape because your mind is trying to protect you, and avoid pain at all costs. Its best course of action is to distract you, and mentally pull you out of your body. This might help in the moment, but it's not so great in the long term because you've completely missed the experience of life in that moment.

Imagine that the energy of the experience freezes, or becomes blocked in your energy system. You haven't allowed yourself to process what happened, and so you've stopped it mid-flow. The energy of the experience remains outside the body. Envisage it being attached to an energetic thread.

We all had lots of negative experiences in our childhoods,

many of which we simply don't remember. The memories have been filed away, and don't remain in our conscious awareness. The mind still believes they're too painful for us to reconnect to, and so we don't remember. Or do we?

They still exist somewhere, deep in our subconscious; the part of the mind that isn't easily accessible to us. The subconscious controls our habits, beliefs, self-image, capabilities and limitations, weaknesses and strengths and our map and model of reality. Our subconscious self is controlling more of our lives than we realise. It stores the masses of unprocessed memories, in which we've pressed pause mid-experience. Be open to the possibility that parts of you are stuck in the past, and these parts contain information frozen in suspended animation all around the outside of your body, within your energy field. This field is alive and pulsating with information. Healers work with this field during sessions, and it gives us the information needed to support you to grow.

In order to continue your healing journey, it's important to work on bringing yourself back into your body. It might bring back some emotional pain, so be prepared.

Tools to help you come back into your body:

1. **RECALL YOUR ENERGY.** Call back your own energy fragments that are littered around the place. Do this now:

   ◆ Sit somewhere quiet (such as your sacred space), close your eyes and take some nice, deep breaths into your body. Place your hands on your thighs, palms facing up to the sky.

- Say out loud: "I call back all of my power, and all of my energy and all of my light from the last week."
- Imagine the energy seeping back into your body. You'll receive whatever's meant for you.
- Breathe the energy back into your hands and heart and lungs and from there feel it spreading out into your cells, and lighting them up as if light were literally spreading out in your body.

It's a good idea to do this at the end of each working day before you head for home.

2. **CONNECT TO YOUR CELLS.** Getting connected to your cellular body is really important. Your biological system is highly intelligent and wants you to heal. When you decide to connect to your cells, you can do it yourself. Here's how I do it:

- Sit somewhere quiet, close your eyes and breathe into your body.
- After a few deep breaths, imagine you can breathe into every single cell in your body.
- Have the intention to breathe into your cells, and imagine your breath connecting with every tiny cell.

3. **CONNECT TO YOUR BONES.** When you ask to connect to a specific part of your body, your body's intelligence will make it happen. Be aware of any self-sabotage such as your conscious brain suggesting it's impossible.

Moving your consciousness into your very bones is the most powerful way of coming into your body. Use the same breathing technique as you did for connecting with your cells.

4. **SIT IN YOUR SEAT.** While in meditation, put your hands on your hips and rest them there. Bring more awareness to your hips and pelvis and breathe into this part of your body. Notice if negative thoughts emerge, or you feel resistance about doing this. If you do sense negativity, simply allow it to be there. Imagine sitting deeper in your seat, and your energy coming into this part of your body. Notice how much stronger you feel now, and own that strength!

5. **BECOME MORE PRESENT.** I have a few techniques that help me to be here instantly, in the moment. Try these:

   ◆ Say out loud: "I'm here!"
   ◆ Stare at your hands, and notice the details, the lines, colours, the textures.
   ◆ Close your eyes and feel your own presence. Be aware of the weight of your body (without judging yourself!). Sense its heaviness and observe your awareness sinking down into it.

Get Connected to Your Higher Self

In this Tonic, you will learn:

♦ About the higher self ♦

♦ About the modern world and the spiritual crisis ♦

♦ Tools to reconnect with your higher self ♦

As mentioned earlier, there are many ways to refer to the higher aspect of us: higher self, higher consciousness, higher power, spirit, divine energy or the universe. Which makes sense to you? Don't worry if you're not sure. Ask yourself the question again when you reach the end of this chapter.

Imagine this higher self like an extension of yourself, which plugs in to a bigger source of divine power, our "source" or "God" (in a spiritual sense). This is our life force, and it channels energy into us that fuels us. It gives us extra oomph, and more zest for life.

As most of us are unaware of our higher self, we don't consciously connect to it, and so we only receive the life force

116

in drips. Our channel or route to connection can be blocked and unused, leaving us spiritually undernourished.

When we're aware of our higher self, and connected to our channel, we can receive more of the life force. Once our channel is open, divine fuel gushes into our lives. We're spiritually abundant and feeding our spirit and souls.

When you open your channel and tune into your higher self, you get:

- instant guidance;
- instant reassurance;
- instant support;
- instant love;
- energy on tap.

You'll feel calmer, freer, more relaxed, supported and held by the mothership! In this chapter, I'm going to explain how you can open up and get connected.

"There is no full life, no fulfilled or meaningful, sustainably joyful life without a connection to the spirit."
– Oprah Winfrey

Are you spiritual?

The higher self is at a higher vibration than the physical human body, so it cannot be seen with our eyes. It's an intangible entity, so requires you to have faith in the unseen – which as we know is difficult at the best of times. In modern society, there's a lot of cynicism about anything that sounds like religion or evokes the concept of spirituality. Unless it can be explained scientifically, we're not willing to accept what we can't see or fully understand.

The word "spirituality" conjures up different ideas, words, feelings or images, depending on your beliefs (or what you've been taught to believe in). It's common to link it to religion and it's common to believe it's "woo-woo" or "out there". You might be feeling resistance as I write about it here.

Many of the world's spiritual leaders think we're experiencing a spiritual crisis globally. We've lost our connection to our higher selves or spirits, the earth and nature. It's as if we're ignoring the fact that we're spiritual beings.

At some point in our history, we became disconnected from the understanding of spirit, soul and energy. There have been many wars and tragedies involving religion and, of course, this information still exists within our ancestral memories, the energy fields of universal consciousness and in the memory fields of our DNA. This could mean we've retained the knowledge at a very deep subconscious level we are completely unaware of. Because the information remains in our system, it still causes fear around spirituality now.

Perhaps there is an underlying fear of spirituality in most of us. I know I felt it for a long time. This suppressed fear is often the reason we close down to an idea, or put obstacles in the way. Without fear, we'd be willing to be open and curious, even if we didn't fully understand, but whenever we experience fear, our minds shut down and we activate the limiting beliefs that control us. They keep us small and closed to new possibilities. Our minds block us from experiencing the higher self, and close the part linked to emotional intelligence and feelings (which is integral to our reconnection). The mind is the only thing standing in our way.

Yet the mind is doing what it believes will ensure our safety and protection, so it's not doing anything wrong. Of course, it's frustrating, but ultimately it's not intending to harm us.

If you're unsure about spirituality and what makes sense to you, you're in a perfectly good place. It's much better to be honest about feeling unclear, sceptical or uncertain. You're then able to work through your feelings in an authentic way until you find your own truths.

I find there's a growing interest in spirituality at the festivals and events that I speak at around the country. There's a great sense of intrigue and a desire to know more. We're waking up to new ways of understanding ourselves because we all want happier lives.

*Take your notebook and write down the words:
Spirituality means . . .*

Then write whatever words come to mind, without judging yourself. When you've finished writing, review what you've written. Notice what comes up for you.

> - How do you feel about it?
> - Do you feel resistance?
> - Or are you open and interested?
>
> This is a great exercise because it's good to get clear about how you feel. Once you're clear, you can address whatever is standing in your way.

We have divine assistance

Let's pause for a moment and take a deep breath in. Do it now.

Is your mind questioning this information?

Are you feeling a little distracted? Want to breeze past this chapter?

Notice if this is you. Catch your mind wandering off. Welcome your resistance.

This isn't meant to overload you, so if it's hard to digest, take it slowly and perhaps make some notes to come back to.

Overseeing or directing our lives is a much bigger task than we realise. Sure, we're creating through our thoughts, beliefs and feelings (there's more on this in Chapter 15) but we need some assistance so the bigger magic can happen. Here's where the divine power comes in.

Imagine a force that is excellent at listening, observing and then assisting us to create what we desire in our lives. The truth is that this is actually happening, and it's readily available for us to use in every moment.

Until we're aware of divine assistance, we aren't taking full advantage of our potential to do incredible things. We are only using a fraction of our human potential, so it's much harder to create from scratch and more energy is required to make things happen. We bumble along in life and blame others for our misfortune when things don't go to plan, or blame ourselves for not being good enough when we don't receive what we want.

All we need to do is be more open to the possibilities. That alone is enough to invite more divine assistance into our lives.

Being powered by divine assistance is like being plugged into a universal power source that offers a turbo boost. It's an upgrade to life. You experience more of life in a richer way, and discover all it has to offer.

The more connected we are to our higher selves and divine assistance, the more we feel we're a part of something. As humans we crave to be connected, and so we yearn to return to this feeling.

Tools to help you get connected:

1. INVITE SPIRIT IN. Practise getting reconnected simply by addressing your higher self, spirit, God (or whichever word works for you) and asking for more intervention in your life. Find a quiet spot (perhaps your sacred space), close your eyes, take a deep breath in and repeat one of these phrases a couple of times: "Dear spirit, thank you for moving through me today" or, "Thank you for loving through me today" or, "Thank you for being here with me today".

Having the intention to let spirit in creates a reconnection in itself. The words "thank you" assume it's already done, and that you expected this to happen. Experiment with the wording that works for you. Interestingly, "God" seems to make the most sense to me in this context.

2. FEED YOUR SPIRIT. Where do you feel most alive? Where do you feel joy and happiness? Is it the park? Is it the beach? Is it the herb garden? Wherever it is, commit to going there as often as possible. The more you go, the more you'll light up, meaning your higher self or spirit is being nourished.

What feeds your soul? Flowers? Poetry? Crystals? Think about how you feel around these things. Surround yourself with objects that switch you on.

3. LISTEN TO UPLIFTING MUSIC. Certain kinds of special music will immediately lift you up. I've suggested a playlist on page 261 but you may have your own favourites that make your soul sing. Make music a part of your daily life.

Create What You Want

> *In this Tonic, you will learn:*
>
> ◆ Basic steps for creating ◆
> ◆ How creation works ◆
> ◆ Tools to assist with creating ◆

As humans we're good at creating physical things in our lives. Our homes, our surroundings, friends and lovers, objects we make. Creating is a natural behaviour, and it's possible because of our energetic nature and the energetic relationship we have with the universe. Because everything around us is energy, everything is connected. Because everything is connected, it is easy for us to attract or create physical things.

How open are you to that idea?

You already have an inner intuition, an understanding that we're all connected. Think about the times when you've thought of someone then soon afterwards seen them walking down the street out of the blue. Or a person's name pops into your mind, then they text or email you immediately afterwards. We've all experienced something like this.

You are able to ask the universe for what you want more of in your life by raising your energetic vibration. When your vibration is higher, you're more aligned to the higher levels of consciousness, or your higher self and divine assistance. In this way you are heard and together you co-create.

How cool is that?

You're able to choose what you want in your life, and then create it!

Is that not brilliant?

You can create the most incredible things for yourself. And your life can be magnificent.

Let's practise creating now.
First we're going to clarify what you want to create in your life. Take out your notebook and write down:

I would like to create . . .

◆ Write what it is you'd like to create. It could be more money or a new relationship, for example.

◆ Get really clear about one or two things you'd like to create and write them down, leaving some space underneath each one.

◆ Next step is to create the feelings associated with what you want to create, and connect these feelings to it.

◆ Write down how you want to feel as you create each thing. Tune into each creation, and really feel it.

◆ For example, imagine that I am looking for a new event space. I need to ask myself how I would feel in the new space. Expansive and limitless? Free and supported? Held and bursting with gratitude for all the people pouring into my workshops? I know I'd feel high because of the energy in the space.

◆ Create these feelings and stay with them, cultivate them. Think about your environment now. Is it supporting these feelings? Are you feeling expansive and limitless and abundant? How can you create these feelings in your environment? One way to create abundance is to be grateful for everything in your life right now. Gratitude raises your energy immediately.

◆ Now you have to learn to let go of whatever you've asked for, send it off into the universe and release your attachment to it. Do this now. Learn to trust that the universe has heard you, and understands what you're asking for.

◆ What you receive won't always look like what you're expecting. The universe knows what is best for you, more than you do. Let it go and send it away with gratitude.

Well done. Now relax and chill out.

The blocks to creating

What's happened in your life lately? New job? New lover? Tax rebate? Break-up? Rejected by your boss? You have created all these things yourself.

As simple as the process sounds so far, there are often blocks that get in the way of creation. Negative and limiting beliefs, fear, tension and resistance all make our vibration remain low. In this state it'll be harder to converse with the universe and to create what we want because we're not engaging the higher consciousness energies and they are not hearing us.

If you don't understand how to create consciously, you end up doing so from a place of fear or neediness. For example: you want a new lover, but deep down you believe you don't deserve love. What happens? No love will come, or you'll meet someone who rejects you and treats you badly. It is easy for us to drop into a feeling of unworthiness, and believe that we don't deserve. Because of this we sabotage our happiness, our wealth, our abundance, our success. The tapping exercise in the Tools at the end of this chapter is specifically designed to deal with blocks to creating.

It is our birthright to be outstanding creators, and to shift our lives to a higher place. As you know by now, we do this by raising our feelings, changing our thoughts and consciously creating a supportive and positive environment.

You deserve to receive everything you desire. A positive step is to claim back your power to create. Use this as a mantra or phrase. Say it right now:

*"I AM an authentic creator and I claim
back my authentic power."*

How do you feel when you say this? Repeat it a few times.

If you feel resistance, doubt or your body tightening or tensing, simply honour your resistance and allow it to be there. It's only here because this is new, unknown territory.

Becoming a conscious creator of your life takes practice and certain qualities: courage, openness, patience, commitment and persistence. We have all these qualities already, but some of them are easier to identify than others.

By far the best way to create more amazing things in your life is to raise your vibes. The higher your vibration, the more good stuff will come to you. Learn to be a lighthouse, full of light and feel-good energy; a person you would want to be around because of their positivity and sparkle.

Tools to offer assistance with creating:

1. HIGH VIBES FIRST THING. Start your day off on a high. This is the time when you can create a higher mood for the rest of your day. If you've had a bad night's sleep, this is a good time to shift your mindset.

- Do a morning meditation session.
- Do some positive affirmations, such as: "I rejoice in the abundance that I am", "I am full of the richness

of life", "I am grateful for all the wealth in my life".
When we use high vibrational words such as rejoice,
richness, wealth and abundance, we raise our natural
vibration. And the words "abundance", "richness"
and "wealth" mean more than money. Extend this
out to think about your life being rich, wealthy and
abundant. Even if you can't see it right now, these
words will create the feelings and raise your energy
levels.

2. GRATITUDE. Keep a gratitude journal in which you write
down all the things that you're grateful for at the end of
each day. Do it for a month and see if you notice any
changes in your energy levels, in things coming into your
life. When you write what you're grateful for, word it in this
way: "I am really grateful for X", or "Thank you so much
for X". Be grateful for good things, bad things and neutral
things!

3. CREATE A GOALS SHEET. Draw this out roughly at first,
then neaten it afterwards. You can use imagery too, to bring
it to life. Split your screen or paper (depending on how you
do it) into different areas of your life that you want to focus
on, such as relationships, career and health, and in each
section paste in images to visually express how you want to
feel, and list two goals that you want to achieve this year.
Write the goals as if you've already achieved them. For
example: "I am completely at peace with my body image",
along with the way you want to feel achieving it, for

example: "I feel free and light in my body". It's really key to hone in on the feeling, and align it with the goal. Tell your partner or a family member or friend what you're doing, and ask them to make you accountable for taking the steps to make your goals happen. When you write things down, you are steering your ship somewhere and have a clearer destination to aim towards.

4. TAP ON RESISTANCE AND RELEASE IT. Take out your notepad to help with this exercise. Tapping will help you with negative beliefs that make you feel you aren't worthy of creating a certain thing. As you're tuning into the feeling of what you want to create and getting clear about it, notice any resistance in your body. It represents fear, and will block you from creating. Tapping is a technique that works with your internal energy meridian system. See the instructions on page 130 for a step-by-step guide.

Let's tap on the general resistance in your body. First of all, focus on what you're feeling resistance towards. Let's say it is creating more wealth in your life (which is a spiritual goal, although you might not think so; money gives you the power to spread more of your light). Rate how much resistance you feel in your body on a scale of 0 to 10 (10 being the most resistance). Write down how you feel about having more wealth. Describe it as clearly as you can. Do you feel guilty about wanting more? Nervous about the responsibility? Worry that you're taking it from someone else? Afraid of being judged?

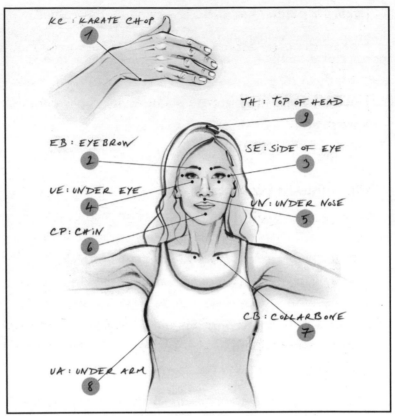

Diagram of tapping points

Take both hands and practise tapping gently with the first three fingers (index, middle and ring fingers) of one hand onto the outside edge of the other. This outside edge point is called the karate-chop point, and this is where we begin the tapping sequence. Say the following phrases out loud while tapping on each of the points listed.

Karate-chop point: "Even though I'm feeling resistance towards my goal, I deeply and completely accept who I am and how I feel." (Repeat three times.)

Eyebrow point: "I'm afraid of having more wealth."

Side of the eye: "When I think about it, I feel tense in my body."

Under the eye: "I'm worried about what people will think of me . . ."

Top lip: ". . . if I receive more wealth."

Chin: "Maybe I don't deserve it."

Collarbone: "Why should I have more wealth?"

Underarm: "It doesn't feel right to want more."

Top of the head: "I'm afraid of having more wealth."

Do a couple of rounds of shorter phrases, until you feel more relaxed about receiving wealth, and then move on to the tapping points below:

Eyebrow point: "I'm willing to let go of this resistance."

Side of the eye: "Holding on doesn't serve me."

Under the eye: "I'm willing to let this go."

Top lip: "And I choose to know I deserve it."

Chin: "I choose to surrender now."

Collarbone: "Holding on doesn't serve me."

Underarm: "I'm a good person."

Top of the head: "And I'm ready to let go, and move into flow."

Do a couple of rounds of this until you feel more positive.

To finish, take some nice, deep breaths in and thank yourself for letting the resistance go, and relaxing more into trust and surrender.

It's Child's Play

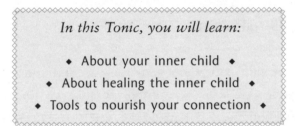

In this Tonic, you will learn:

♦ About your inner child ♦
♦ About healing the inner child ♦
♦ Tools to nourish your connection ♦

We talked about your inner child in earlier chapters but now it's time to explore the concept further. Your inner child is an aspect of you that still represents you the way you were in childhood. We remain incredibly influenced by who we were as children. We hold onto old memories of experiences we went through: the pain of being rejected, left behind, ignored, abandoned . . . We all have our own stories and our own scars. We all have memories we've blocked and hidden away because we don't want to relive the pain and the trauma.

Your inner child experienced your earliest emotional memories and pain, so now forms the essence of your emotional body. If you are disconnected from your emotions now, it's because you haven't learned how to heal your inner child.

133

The experiences and the wounds from childhood form the foundations of who we are as people now. They're the reason we behave a certain way, such as sabotaging our relationships and career prospects.

——

Essentially, we're all wounded children walking around in adults' bodies.

——

Healing the inner child

Your inner child represents your fundamental core memories and experiences, so is very important to you. Reconnect to your inner child, and you gain new insight and understanding from the past, and you can heal on a very deep level.

Your inner child is a vital piece of your healing puzzle, holding many gifts for your transformation.

The main way to heal your child is by connection. He or she is a part of you, so is ready and waiting for you to connect with her, communicate with her regularly and nourish this relationship. Imagine your inner child as a lost little orphan who feels frightened and abandoned. The reconnection or healing process has three main steps, as follows (I've used the word "she" to refer to the child but this applies equally to men and women):

1. **GAIN HER TRUST.** She's scared and doesn't trust anyone, especially you. You disconnected from her and abandoned

her when she needed you the most. You will have to win her trust again.

2. REGULAR CONTACT. This can't be a one-hit wonder, or something you do when you occasionally remember. To create a fulfilling and nourishing relationship with her, you have to have regular contact and dialogue.

3. COMMIT TO HER NEEDS. As part of growing this relationship, it's important that you commit to understanding her needs and making sure you meet them. This might involve jumping on the swing in the park, or buying an ice cream or eating CocoPops for breakfast . . . (Don't worry, you can negotiate – but it has to be on her terms.)

When you heal the connection between you and your inner child, life becomes fun again. You remember what it was like to see the world through a child's eyes. Life turns into a big game, and feels light and playful. You're naturally more curious about the world around you. It's important to develop curiosity, because the energy of curiosity opens up many doors that might have been closed to you before.

Why we're disconnected from our inner children

What does your average week consist of? Working late, emails, more work?

Adult life can be mundane, boring and joyless. Full of grown-up responsibilities: relationship problems, financial struggles and debt, meeting deadlines, working overtime, stress and lots of hard work.

Most of us have lost our connection to our inner child, and life has gradually become more serious. We're weighed down by the heaviness of adult life. If we only have one life (that we know of), don't we need to have more fun and be happier and make the most of it?

You used to be curious, playful and carefree. What happened? What changed?

You grew up. You left your child behind. You became serious and mature.

You now have many more things on your mind, but that doesn't need to mean you lose the fun in life. If you reconnect to your inner child, you connect back to those qualities, and life becomes fun again.

It doesn't matter if you're a lawyer or a banker or a DJ: you're still a child inside.

This little child is waiting for you to reach out and tell her you love her. So do it. Make time for her. Be loving to her

Right now she's a little pissed off. She's been waiting a very long time for you. As you moved into adulthood, you left your child behind. So she sits waiting for you, feeling forgotten and abandoned.

She's lost her sparkle, she's dimmed her light and is in a bit of a huff!

And you don't speak to her in a very loving way. You scold her, you tell her she's not good enough, not pretty enough, not thin enough. When you talk down to yourself, you're talking down to her.

Your child doesn't care about your fears and worries, if the new boyfriend is going to call or not, how many calories you ate for lunch, how many chocolate biscuits you had in your tea break. All she wants is fun, play and excitement with you.

When you integrate the inner child, your life will become more joyful. She's waiting for you, so go and connect. But before you rush in, know this: she might be hiding and she might be afraid.

This is an exercise of persistence, practice and no expectation. She needs patience and understanding from you, in order to rebuild the trust. You're dealing with a little child, even though she isn't visible to you as a physical one.

The good news is she will forgive, forget and brush herself off, as all children do. She wants to be with you again; she's desperate for your company. So what are you waiting for?

Commit to the practice of befriending your inner child.

If you think you don't have time to do this, make time. This is one of the most important stages of your healing journey.

___

Heal your connection with your inner child and life will become more fun and playful.

___

Fun and play are important to your development because they ignite your spirit, light you up and lift your vibration – all of which are essential for creating a better life.

When you have a good connection with your inner child, she'll flow through into your everyday life. You'll have richer experiences, and flourish. Worries will diminish, and negative thoughts will float through you, without sticking.

The most radical transformations I've seen in clients have come from healing the inner child. She holds the keys to your transformation, and when you work with the childhood memories, big changes will happen.

Tools to nourish your inner child:

1. HANG OUT WITH HER. Chat to your inner child, and ask her what she wants to do today. Listen for a response and then honour what you receive by doing it. For example, she might tell you she wants to go to the park. Can you visit the park today? If you can't, compromise with her. Tell her you promise to go at the weekend, or that you'll walk around a garden instead. If you promise to go at the weekend, you have to go. Oh, and if you don't hear a response from your inner child at first, keep practising until you do. It will happen.

2. BE INTIMATE WITH HER. Use a mirror to connect deeply. Look into the mirror, breathe into your heart and connect through your eyes. In doing this, you're connecting with her. When you speak to yourself in the mirror, you're really speaking to her. Hold the eye contact for a while, even if you feel uncomfortable doing it. Allow yourself to experience the feelings. Take some deep breaths. Appreciate her and how special she is. Talk to her either in your mind, or out loud if you're alone. Tell her you love her. Tell her you'll always be available to her. Tell her she's the most important person in your life. Tell her how special she is to you. Tell her you're here for her. If you feel emotional, allow tears to flow. Persist with this; it's a very powerful way of healing your child.

3. TAP ON THE CHILDHOOD PAIN AND RELEASE IT. In the last chapter, I explained that tapping is a technique that works with your internal energy meridian system.

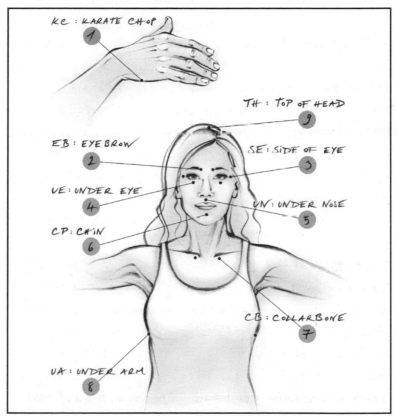

Diagram of tapping points

Let's tap on the old childhood feelings remaining in your body. As you connect with your inner child, and become more intimate with her, make a note of what she is feeling. You can get a good indication of her childhood wounds this way. Notice the most powerful feelings, such as rejection. Ask yourself: how rejected do I feel on a scale of 0 to 10 (with 10 being the most rejected). Select a number and rate the rejection.

Practise tapping gently with the first three fingers (index, middle and ring fingers) of one hand on the karate-chop point while repeating the phrases below.

Karate-chop point: "Even though I still feel rejected, I deeply and completely accept who I am and how I feel." (Repeat three times.)

Eyebrow point: "I still feel rejected."

Side of the eye: "It's a big wound for me."

Under the eye: "I feel tense in my heart."

Top lip: "When I talk about this rejection . . ."

Chin: ". . . all this rejection . . ."

Collarbone: ". . . that I'm holding on to . . ."

Underarm: "Why am I still holding on?"

Top of the head: "This feeling of rejection, it's still here."

Do a couple of rounds of the shorter phrases, until you feel better about the rejection, and then move on:

Eyebrow point: "I'm willing to let go."

Side of the eye: "Holding on doesn't serve me."

Under the eye: "I'm willing to let this go . . ."

Top lip: ". . . and I choose to relax more."

Chin: "I choose to surrender now."

Collarbone: "Holding on doesn't serve me."

Underarm: "I'm a good person."

Top of the head: "And I'm ready to let go."

Do a couple of rounds of this, until you feel more positive.

To finish, take some nice, deep breaths in and thank yourself for letting this go.

4. WATCH ANIMATED PIXAR OR DISNEY MOVIES. Your inner child likes watching movies with fairies, superheroes, princesses, animals, toys and any other you liked as a child. Re-visit all the golden oldies. You'll secretly love them all over again.

5. READ CHILDREN'S BOOKS. Any fantasy children's books like Harry Potter. Have a look around your local bookshop and lose yourself in a magical world.

CHAPTER

17

Heal Your Heart

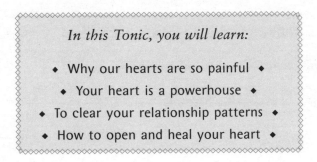

In this Tonic, you will learn:

- ◆ Why our hearts are so painful ◆
- ◆ Your heart is a powerhouse ◆
- ◆ To clear your relationship patterns ◆
- ◆ How to open and heal your heart ◆

Ever had your heart broken?

Of course you have, and it's agonising. Imagine someone stomping all over your heart with their big, heavy boots. You are crushed, you feel worthless and insignificant. Life is so bad that the world could be ending and you wouldn't even care. You want it to end; there's no point carrying on. If the world doesn't end, you might end it yourself right now. It's all so hopeless; you feel the pain of being unloved and rejected right in your heart's core.

You're in a deep, dark hole and there's no light, not even a crack.

After a good ol' stint at life with all its testing experiences, the heart is scarred, heavy and weighed down with emotion.

Wounded from battle, we feel tender and beaten up. Carrying a ton of old emotion, the heart feels painful and we don't want to connect to it. We fear the darkness inside, and what we'll find when we open it up. So we shut down this part of ourselves and become comfortably numb. We disconnect from our memories and build a force-field around the heart.

We enter into relationships which are either very **safe**, so as not to trigger the old pain, or very **unsafe** because we hope that by repeating the same thing over and over we will eventually find a different outcome and thus heal the pain. Either way we're closed down completely, so it's no wonder the relationships we find are lacking in the love we crave.

Lugging the baggage around

Most of the pain we carry is very old, and comes from early traumatic memories.

Imagine this: you're a little child in nursery, and one day Mummy forgets to pick you up. You're the last one standing, with the teacher and the tumbleweed. In that moment, you're forgotten and abandoned by the person you trust to keep you safe and protected. At the time, the experience is too painful to process and you don't fully understand what's happening. As a coping mechanism, you freeze the experience and file the memory somewhere deep inside the subconscious mind. Somewhere you can't access it. You form the belief that you're unwanted and unloved.

Imagine this: you're born prematurely and placed in an incubator. You lie in a protective box that keeps you warm and oxygenated but you are isolated from human connection. We need connection and love from other humans; it keeps us alive. Science has proven that newborn babies can die or become very weak and fragile if they're not stroked when in incubators. You remember the emotional starvation, and you remember the disconnection and abandonment. You form the belief that you're unwanted and unlovable.

Early memories such as these contribute to the deep emotional pain we hold onto now.

When we're disconnected from our hearts, we don't know how to feel the heart or connect to it. We don't realise this disconnection has happened until our heart gets broken again. Then we're reminded, and feel it crumble once more.

No wonder we associate our hearts with pain. It doesn't help when musicians describe their broken hearts in their latest tracks. Broken hearts for everyone. It's drummed into our psyche how painful our hearts can be.

But here's the good news (drumroll please): the heart is a mighty brain.

What we're not taught at school is how powerful the heart actually is. Imagine the heart as a brain, with 40,000 neurones that detect circulating hormones and neurochemicals. The heart is the most powerful generator of electromagnetic energy in the body, about 60 times greater in amplitude than the electrical activity generated by the brain, according to the HeartMath Research Center. It's the centre of pure emotions such as: love, joy, appreciation; and based on the idea that our emotion creates our reality, the purer our emotion, the clearer (and less complicated) our reality.

Your heart has the power to create more happiness in your life. You've heard the term "lionheart"? These words combined reinforce the courageousness of the heart. The dictionary definition is "a person of exceptional courage and bravery". Imagine your heart as your inner lion, a big force deep inside you that wants to express itself and isn't afraid to do so.

If this is all true, why don't we automatically work in harmony with the heart?

Because the mind gets in the way, again. Its role is to protect us by keeping us safe and pain-free. It won't let us connect to the heart because of all that old pain. The mind is good at keeping us away from anything that feels unsafe.

But as with so many other things, you have a choice. If you want to grow, you can choose a braver, more heart-centred life.

Decision time

There are two options:

- Ignore this revolutionary information, and stay small and hidden. You are in pain (even if you don't realise it) and this pain is waiting behind the scenes to emerge at some point in your life.

Or

- Choose to move bravely into the heart. It might be painful at first, but the pain will be short-lived and intense (like ripping off a plaster). And – this is the best bit – the heart actually wants you to heal so it'll work with you, so you get what you need and heal faster.

Which will you choose?

I'm hoping it's the second option, because I want you to heal. On some level you want to know more; you wouldn't be reading this book otherwise. Remember: I've been here before, I know the journey and I can tell you it's sometimes difficult but, ultimately, pretty incredible.

> *Pause for a moment and think about your relationships so far. Are you good at inviting in heartbreak? Do you repeat the same patterns? Do you get more and more frustrated each time it happens?*
>
> ◆ A good place to start is thinking about what your partners most often moan about. What do they want to change about you? Are there any things that come up time and again?
>
> ◆ Next, think about how you commonly feel in your relationships. What are the painful emotions you experience? Rejection, feeling unloved, abandoned, betrayed, left out?
>
> ◆ List the pain points now. Don't over-analyse; simply allow yourself to make a list.
>
> ◆ Getting clear on the main problem areas in your relationships is a powerful first step. Clarity = power. Simply by becoming more aware, you'll notice when they next arise, and identify the triggers. Because many of these patterns are locked in our subconscious, we tend to repeat them without

realising and will often sabotage new relationships without being aware of what we're
doing or having any idea how to change our
behaviour.

◆ You can have all the best intentions –
perhaps finding someone new who isn't like
your previous partners – but if you don't shift
your subconscious pain, before long the same
patterns will be played out.

◆ Shifting the pain means you'll feel more
confident in letting your guard down, and
inviting more love in. You have to get to a
place of feeling safer and more healed to
enable you to do this.

Tools to heal your heart:

1. RECONNECT TO YOUR HEART. Put your hand on your
heart. Breathe into this place. Connect to your heart. Feel
the heartbeat. How does your heart feel? Tight? Painful?
Keep breathing into it. Are you a visual person? I like to
think of the heart as a beautiful rose with many layers of
petals. It isn't simply an organ; it's so much more. Breathe
into the layers of petals.

2. OPEN YOUR HEART. You can make a conscious decision
simply to open your heart. You might not believe it's

possible to do this, but in the same way you close your heart down when you feel threatened, you can make the choice to open it instead. Your heart listens and responds to you, so you can open it by asking yourself to. It might feel a little overwhelming or wobbly at first. I remember opening my heart this way, and I felt a little vulnerable and powerless for a moment before getting used to it. Because of this, it's a good idea to practise this in a meditation on your own in a safe place, such as your sacred space. Here's what to do:

- Close your eyes.
- Breathe into your heart.
- Say slowly to yourself, "I open my heart" and feel your way into the words.
- Repeat this over and over until you feel comfortable.

3. SHIFT THE BARRIERS. We all have a protective wall surrounding our hearts, and it's up to us to shift it somehow. Visualisation is a good way to do this. Sit quietly somewhere, close your eyes and relax. Focus your awareness on your heart. Visualise the wall around your heart. Can you sense it? If you're immediately putting a barrier in the way of doing this, honour your resistance and see if you can sense it again. Imagine the wall all around your heart, surrounding you. How does it feel? What colour is it? Bring it to life in your mind. Creating it in your mind will make it more visible to you. When you sense more of a connection to your wall, bring more awareness to it and imagine that you're feeling into it and reaching out to touch it. Next, in a few big, deep and powerful breaths, breathe the wall into your heart for transformation. Repeat this for five to ten minutes every morning for a week and see if you can notice any difference. How much easier is it to open your heart now, as in Tool 2 above?

4. STRAIGHT FROM THE HEART. Use your mirror for this. Prepare a little first: place your hand over your heart and take some deep breaths into your heart to get more connected. Face yourself in the mirror, look into your eyes and let your heart speak. Tell yourself how much you love yourself, and how sorry you are for being away for so long. Keep breathing into your heart even if it hurts. You will move through the pain. Really let yourself talk and express from your heart. It's very cleansing!

Body Talks

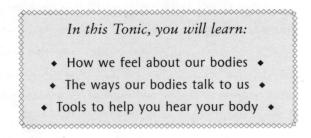

In this Tonic, you will learn:

- ◆ How we feel about our bodies ◆
- ◆ The ways our bodies talk to us ◆
- ◆ Tools to help you hear your body ◆

How do you feel about your body?

As the question sinks in, you might inhale a big gulp of air and go silent. Your brain is trying its best to find the right words. You spend a few minutes trying to condense ten negative thoughts into one sentence that sums up perfectly what you think and believe about your body.

When the question is "How do you feel about something?" it's an invitation to tune into your feelings, which are sensed in your body. Because we're so disconnected from our feelings, and we've not been taught how to feel, this is an alien concept to us. The mind quickly intervenes and thinks up a logical response that's much safer to give.

If we actually tuned in to our feelings about our bodies,

it's likely we'd feel tension, resistance and underlying pain. Why? Because we all have negative perceptions of our bodies. Too bold a statement? I haven't yet met anyone who loves all of their body. Even if you've worked hard to tone and perfect your body, you'll still have underlying issues. It's unlikely you've released the underlying emotions linked to how you feel.

We see our bodies through a critical lens. The way we see ourselves when we face the mirror is very different to how our friends, lovers or family see us.

We hold many body memories in our subconscious. Maybe we were teased for having "puppy fat", or heard a teenage boy we fancied talking about our fat thighs, or a boyfriend telling us we'd be better if we lost some weight (as happened to me). Even though these conversations seemed more or less harmless at the time, we hold onto the memory and associated emotions of being "fat" or "not slim enough". We remember all the images of the "perfect body" portrayed in magazines. From this, we construct an ideal body image, which we can never match up to.

Burdened with all of these old memories and reasons why our bodies aren't good enough, we create negative beliefs about our bodies.

Q: Which part of your body do you love the most?

◆ Take a moment to ask yourself this question, and write down the answer. Take all the time you need, and if there's more than one, list them all.

◆ By the way, it's **not** OK to skip this part, or tell yourself you don't know. If you were sitting across from me right now, I'd easily list five parts of your body that are beautiful. Stop being so hard on yourself and answer the question!

◆ Now I want you to write down a reason why you love it (or them). Write the reason next to your body part, and be as descriptive as possible.

For example: I love my back. I love how it curves, and flows from the top of my neck, all the way down to my bottom. I love my defined spine, which shows the spinal bones running down my back. I love it when my back is exposed. It feels sexy.

Q: Which part of your body do you dislike the most?

◆ Take a moment to decide which part of your body you most dislike and write it down. Start with one body part and be gentle. Don't give yourself any more reasons to hate your body; you do enough of that already.

◆ Now I want a reason why you dislike it. Write the reason next to your body part, being as descriptive as possible, and as honest as you can. For example: I dislike my stomach. It feels heavy, like a tyre that sticks out and runs all around my torso.

My digestive system doesn't work properly, and my stomach is always bloated. I constantly look around at other people's flat stomachs and I wish I had a tummy like that.

◆ All done? Good. Now take a look at the part you dislike most and reframe your belief by suggesting something positive. For example: my tummy is a vital part of my body; my digestive system processes all the food I eat to create more energy to fuel me. Give it a try.

Once you've done this, repeat with any other body parts you dislike, but be gentle!

Your body is intuitive and it hears you

The body knows when you dislike it. It senses the negativity and absorbs it into the cells, muscles, tissues and blood. When you focus on negative thoughts about a body part, your mind releases energy in the form of emotions, which are projected into the part and stay there. The more negative thoughts you have, the more energy you send there, and the more solid the beliefs.

———

Your body is suffering because of your past experiences, and the beliefs and feelings you've created around them.

———

How do you feel about your body now? A little bit guilty? What's your body ever done to you? Its purpose is to support you and function on your behalf. To be the physical aspect: strong, solid and healthy.

Your body suffers because your mind causes the suffering. There's no point feeling guilty about how you've treated your body in the past. Wake up now and become responsible for your thoughts, emotions and actions about your body.

The body communicates through sensations: pains, tension, aches, niggles and twitches. We're so removed from this idea that whenever we experience pain in our bodies, we react and get angry, afraid or frustrated. This creates more negativity and adds to the pain. To fix it? We're trained to take the nearest painkiller rather than listening to our bodies and understanding what they are telling us. We numb the pain completely, and aim to shut it down. Does this sound like the best thing to do?

The body is very literal in explaining what's wrong. It often seems to communicate with us via certain parts that correspond to specific topics we're struggling with. Here are some examples of how the body communicates with us by expressing discomfort or pain in a certain area. These are direct experiences I've had with clients:

♦ Tension or pain in the lower back/lumbar-spine area corresponds to a belief that you are unsupported in life. It's usually from childhood, and is how you felt around your parents. It's common if your parents worked away, or weren't able to connect with you emotionally; for example, if they were workaholics or alcoholics.

◆ Tension or pain in the knees means a feeling of being stuck in life, or a fear of moving towards something. You literally feel unable to move forwards.

◆ Tension or pain in your shoulders means a feeling of being burdened by something in your life. Perhaps by your parents, or by other responsibilities you've agreed to take on.

Our bodies want us to understand what's happening and so will try and communicate in the most obvious way they know how. Because we're not trained in listening, it's difficult for us to hear and understand.

Body trauma

The body holds onto memories of trauma. We store the emotional aspects and negative memories in our cells, muscles, tissues and blood. If something has happened to a specific body part, we'll hold the information of what happened. For example, if you fall off your bike as a child and cut your knee open, you'll retain the memories of the pain and the trauma in your knee. You'll hold onto this until you have an opportunity to let it go, usually in a healing or meditation session.

It's very common to hold onto the belief "It's not safe to be in my body" in your subconscious mind. I mentioned earlier how we escape the body during times of trauma, and disconnect from ourselves (see page 112). When this happens numerous times, we create a belief system. It becomes our truth, and we'll avoid being in the body because we believe it's not safe. This belief is very common with sufferers of eating disorders and survivors of abuse.

Another common behaviour is protecting ourselves by retaining the fatty tissue in a certain area. For example, it's common to hold onto weight in the stomach because you are literally trying to be bigger so there's more of you to help protect yourself. Obesity and extreme weight gain are usually a sign of unprocessed childhood trauma.

It may be difficult to rid yourself of old trauma but your body is highly intelligent and knows how to detoxify. When you're releasing the old information, your body will clear out old emotions. This means that you'll feel more tired than usual, you might have a sore throat or a cold, and you will certainly feel emotional. This process is positive as you're removing it rather than letting it fester on the inside.

Your body is tougher than you think. A psychic once told me that we all choose our bodies (she called it a "body suit") based on what's going to be happening to us in our lives. I'm open to the possibility. Why not? It keeps me open to the belief that my body is more than equipped to deal with whatever life throws my way.

Your body is beautiful. Embrace every curve, every wrinkle, every scar, every mark. These are all symbols of who you are and what you've made it through.

Tools to help you hear your body:

1. GET UP CLOSE AND PERSONAL. Get naked and stand in front of a mirror. What are you telling yourself as you look into that mirror? Which parts of your body are you sending negativity to? Become aware of how you are talking to yourself, and your body parts. Notice that you're sending negative energy to different parts of your body.

2. REFRAME YOUR NEGATIVITY. Re-visit the list you wrote earlier, focusing on the parts of your body you dislike, and reframe each one so you find a positive reason to accept and love yourself again.

3. PARTY WITH PAIN. When you next feel pain, rather than reaching for the Nurofen, why not sit somewhere quiet and close your eyes. Take some nice, deep breaths into your body and move your focus to the pain. Sit with the pain and start to become curious about what your body is feeling. Usually behind the pain is blocked energy or emotion, so all you need to do is breathe into it and have the intention to "let it go". You might need to sit with the pain for a few minutes. Be patient and tell yourself you have all the time in the world. It's not always about the quick fix.

4. PRESS INTO PAIN. When you feel tightness and knots in your shoulders or anywhere else in the body, use the tips of your fingers to press into the pain, and take a deep breath in at the same time. You'll experience the breath going right up into the tightness, and oxygen being taken into the muscle tension to loosen it. I haven't used any painkillers for five years, because I've realised that pain can be released naturally. I haven't suffered any chronic pain or terminal illness so I'm not dismissing the use of painkillers in these circumstances, but for mild headaches, toothache, earache and stomach ache, it is possible to release these pains easily. See if you can!

Get More Love

In this Tonic, you will learn:

* ◆ What love means to you ◆
* ◆ How to love yourself more ◆
* ◆ Tools to get more love ◆

What is love?

Take a few minutes to think about this now. Grab your notebook and pen, write down "What is love?" at the top, and then list everything that you relate to love. Let the words flow without judging yourself. It's important to be honest; only you will see this.

How did you get on? Are you surprised by what you wrote down?

When I first did this exercise a few years ago, my words were: vulnerable, closed, blocked, intense, painful, fear, unsafe.

It was immediately obvious that I had negative associations with love. I remembered the trail of broken relationships behind me and I felt sad. Back then, I yearned for love and desired a healthy, clean connection to it, something I'd not yet experienced. I realised I would have to face my emotional baggage and my past experiences if I was to receive the type of love I craved.

You'll naturally relate love to emotional experiences with the people close to you, such as your mum, dad, siblings, early partners. Without realising it, you'll base your definition of love on these past experiences. If you've come through painful encounters, even if the person concerned didn't mean to hurt you, they'll be logged as distressing memories, and become evidence to reinforce your current beliefs about love.

It's important not to blame anyone for what happened to you. In every moment, we believe we're doing the best we can. We all tend to behave in the way we learned to behave as children, based on the way we were treated. **What's important now is to recognise the pain you're holding onto, and work through it with an open heart and a willingness to let go of the past.** Holding onto blame and resentment keeps you very stuck and rigid. The Tools at the end of this chapter will help you to let go.

Love is an experience

We're very keen to define love. In fact, the question "What is love?" was the most Googled phrase in 2012, and it was back at no. 3 in 2014.

As an explorer of love for the past six years, I've realised that it's not at all easy to define. Love means something different to everyone:

- If you're a baby, love means Mummy, Daddy, milk, nourishment, warmth.
- If you're a dog, love means food, a snuggly blanket, praise when you bring the ball back.
- If you're an orphan or homeless, love might not exist for you at all.

We all have contrasting interpretations of love, depending on what we've experienced and what we've been taught. We have different love stories and different love topics. It's very confusing when we move into a new relationship. If you've had challenging relationships in the past, your love story might be of abandonment and rejection. It's likely you'll then push love away, because you don't want to get hurt again. The prospect of love is too painful, and yet because you yearn for love you'll keep inviting it in.

Your first experience of love is your birth. When you're born into this world, the first thing you feel (usually) is love and connection from your mother. If the birth goes smoothly, you'll immediately connect with your mother and feel a loving bond. You'll feel safe, loved and supported.

If there are complications, the first thing you might pick up is the panic, fear and anxiety of your mother, the nurses and whoever else is in the room. No matter how experienced the professionals, they're only human and can still feel panic as they try to remedy the situation. When this happens, it's possible to absorb the negative energy. If the birth was traumatic, your mother might not feel an instant love or connection with you, and you'll absorb this fear and lack of love.

If you were an unwanted child – an "accident" – you can

absorb your mother's thoughts and emotions through the umbilical cord while still in the womb. You'll emerge into the world and subconsciously feel the rejection and disconnection from her love.

It's common to experience complications or trauma during birth. The good news is you can heal these memories, even the most traumatic. I've experienced many deep healing sessions for birth trauma through my work as a healer. Even as tiny babies, we are all more resilient than we think.

Negative associations with love

Did you write any negative words in answer to the question "What is love?"

This is very common. Some people associate love with control and manipulation; their experience of love is that it's conditional – they only receive it in return for doing something the other person wants.

Here's one scenario I see in my practice. Imagine your parents divorced when you were five years old and, for some reason, your mum decided to walk out and leave you with your dad. Perhaps your dad was so overcome with loss and sadness, he used you as bait to emotionally manipulate your mum, in an attempt to lure her home. You might not be able to remember every detail, but we're very sensitive as children, so you absorbed the negative energy and fear surrounding the divorce. As this was your early experience of love, it formed the foundations upon which you base your current associations with love. Without realising it, you have created the belief system that love is controlling and manipulative. Fast forward to the present day, and you attract controlling and manipulative relationships.

We all copy patterns from our parents. You might not be aware of this pattern, and it's possible it won't be visible in all of your relationships, but you can be sure that most of them will show the signs. It's common to be in denial or not realise the cycles or patterns you are caught up in. As brilliant as we are at seeing what we want to see when we want to see it, we're also great at not seeing what we need to see.

Love is a big and powerful energy force

We're all searching for love, whether we know it or not. We all want to feel love, and we yearn for it in the purest form.

———

Experiencing pure love is the highest of the high and, when we're feeling this, all our fears melt away.

———

We're vibrant, alive, ecstatic, light and happier than we've ever been. Pure love is a spiritual experience that we yearn for.

Imagine love as a flow of energy you can connect to. It's a type of formless, limitless energy dancing around your body. Yes, it's something you can give to others and receive in return, but the purest form is energy. Imagine love is inside you and all around you. Love is energy and so are you. In your natural state, you are love.

If love is all around us and within us, why don't we feel it all the time?

Because of fear, which is the opposite of love in every way. Fear stops us from experiencing and feeling love. Fear blocks the magic of love from happening. We live our lives in fear. We've inherited fear, and we've learned about fear since childhood. Fear keeps us hidden and small, and blocked from receiving the love we deserve and were born to receive.

Fear also keeps us safe. Opening up to receive love feels unsafe. It means vulnerability and we're afraid of letting our guards down. It's easier to shut love out than let love in.

Our mission in life is to move out of fear and into love. That is the key here: to move into love.

How do we do that?

Self-love. We have to learn how to love ourselves, and make it a big part of the journey.

- The more you love you, the more you can love others.
- The more you love you, the more others can love you.
- The more you love you, the more you open up to universal love.
- The more you love you, the more good stuff happens.

Do you need any more reasons?

Already loving yourself? Great! Keep going. There's always more work to do; it's an ongoing love mission.

Or does the mention of self-love make you cringe? If so, you absolutely need to do this. What you're feeling is resistance towards loving yourself.

Have you been raised to believe that it's selfish or arrogant to focus on you? Do you dislike yourself as a person? I'm hoping the answer is no – although it might feel like it sometimes. We tend to keep scorecards on ourselves and each time we get something "wrong" (in our eyes), we silently beat ourselves up for it. There's this mean inner boss in all of us who thinks she's in charge, and she berates us all the time. She dishes out punishments and she rules us through fear. But it doesn't have to be this way. It's high time we reclaimed our power from her, because she's been ruling the roost for far too long.

The more resistance you feel, the more you need to do this, so invite the resistance along for the ride and get going. You need to become your own biggest fan and cheer yourself on, just as you cheer on your best mates.

Why would you **not** allow yourself to be proud of all your achievements?

Why would you **not** love yourself and all you've become?

You are amazing!

Tools to get more love:

1. **GIVE MORE LOVE.** Quite simply, you'll receive more love through giving more love. Where are you not giving love freely and easily in your life? Your personal relationships? With your work colleagues?

Why are you holding your love back? Do you believe it's weak to show love? Do you withhold love to teach people a lesson? Do you hold back because they don't deserve it? Are you waiting until someone does something for you before giving them love?

Notice where you're holding yourself back from giving love, and make a conscious effort to dish out more: more compliments, more smiles, more affection. When we give out love, it raises our vibration and we receive love back.

2. RELEASE OLD EMOTIONS. Find somewhere quiet and comfortable (perhaps your sacred space) and sit down. Close your eyes and take some deep breaths into your body. Take time to relax your mind then move your awareness into your body. Your intention is to connect to the energy and emotions of your relationships as a whole. Don't overthink this; simply become aware of any sensations that begin to stir in your body. Imagine that you're holding a healing space for yourself, as if you're supporting yourself like you would a child, by being present and solid for them. Witness the feelings and emotions that arise. You can step closer and notice more and then step away again if you need to. Think to yourself: "This is simply energy moving through." When we detach and move away, the old emotions will shift and pass gently through. If you feel anything tight or knotted coming up, do the same. Become more aware but don't panic; simply allow it to pass through you.

3. STEP INTO THE ENERGY FIELD. Find a clear space with no clutter around. Take a blank sheet of A4 paper and write down the word "relationships" in big, clear writing. Place the sheet of paper on the floor in the middle of the space. Stand up and step back a few steps from the paper. In doing this, you have created an energy field of relationships. You are now going to walk very slowly towards the paper. It's important you walk slowly because I want you to become aware of how your body responds as you move into the energy field of relationships. If you rush this, you'll miss your responses. With every step that you take towards the paper, you might feel more sensations or emotions arising. When you reach the paper, gently step on it with both feet. Stand in the middle of the paper, close your eyes and take some deep breaths. Notice the sensations in your body. You might feel emotional as old energies move and change inside you. When you feel something, pause so you become fully aware of it then step away and allow it to release. To help you release you can use a phrase such as "I choose to release this now" or "I choose to let go of this now". These will act as positive instructions, making it easier to let go.

4. I LOVE YOU, I HEART YOU. Look in a mirror and tell yourself: "I love you." To release any resistance you have about doing this (it's hard at first), make a fist and tap gently on the V in the middle of your collarbone. Repeat a few times. This is a brilliant way of affirming your love for yourself.

5. DATE YOU. What do you love doing? Where do you love going? Plan the perfect date for yourself – just you, not you and your partner. If you feel weird about doing this alone, start with something small like going to watch a movie you want to see or visit an exhibition of work by your favourite artist. Commit to dating yourself at least once a month. This is time for you, and you alone.

Feel Your Feelings

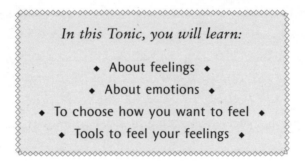

In this Tonic, you will learn:

- ◆ About feelings ◆
- ◆ About emotions ◆
- ◆ To choose how you want to feel ◆
- ◆ Tools to feel your feelings ◆

How are you feeling right now?

Feelings are felt in the body. Let's move into your body and observe how you're feeling. Be as honest as possible about everything that's going on with you.

Take out your notepad and write down: "I am feeling . . ."

Place your hand over your heart, close your eyes, breathe into your heart a few times, while asking yourself the question: "How am I feeling?"

Write down the words that come to you; for example, tight, tense, angry, open, happy, tired.

Don't worry how you sound; just allow the words to flow. This is your exercise and no one else will see it.

Watch out for your mind getting in the way. We are all prone to processing things in our minds first, but the mind doesn't feel. The heart and body feel. The mind gets in the way and questions what you're feeling, and then you get stuck.

Make sense? This is much harder than it sounds but if you persevere you will get there.

Understanding feelings

Do you understand what feelings are?

This isn't a trick question; it's a very real one. There are many definitions of feelings, depending on where you look for the answer.

When a feeling is experienced, you'll feel it in your body as a physical response. A feeling is felt in the heart and body as an immediate reaction to outside stimuli. The mind is not involved at that stage, but the heart and body are. Feelings happen without any judgement from the mind, because a feeling is experienced before the mind is involved. Imagine a feeling as a pre-thought experience.

If you're feeling a little lost right now, don't worry. The most important thing is to get you experiencing feelings again.

Imagine a beautiful interior-design shop full of different fabrics and textures. Some feel luxurious and silky, while others feel coarse and threadbare. This represents the wealth of feelings inside us. We have access to all these types of feelings. In every moment we can decide how we want to feel.

When we react to something and it doesn't feel good, we don't have to stay with the feeling. We can decide to exchange it and feel something else instead. We always have a choice.

This is a revelation, because it's hard for us to believe that we can choose what to feel.

Again, we always have a choice. It may not seem like it all the time, but we do. We live in a universe of free will, and that means choosing what we want to do, feel and think.

The history of the world is full of great "thinkers" who solved problems using the mind. In childhood, we're taught to use the mind as the primary brain, and so we naturally do this without being fully conscious of it. We give the mind tasks to do and problems to solve. But the mind can only give us advice or thoughts based on past experience, and the lessons we've learned from those experiences.

Imagine you're preparing to give a talk to a big audience. The mind will automatically connect to memories from your past when you felt pain or humiliation in a similar situation: maybe you forgot your script or made a mistake or stumbled as you walked up to the microphone. Because of these negative experiences, the mind will switch into safety mode and do its best to stop you giving the talk. You'll experience anxiety, fear and procrastination, which are all barriers to prevent you from speaking. As annoying as this sounds, the mind is fulfilling its primary function: to keep you safe and protected. It isn't doing anything wrong; in fact, it's trying to help.

Using the mind as our primary brain creates limitations. The more we do so, the more disconnected we are from the feelings or "intuition" coming from the hearts and bodies. There's a worldwide misunderstanding of what feelings are but I'm here to tell you that we can change our lives for the better when we learn to experience feelings more.

While researching feelings to better understand why we've become detached from them, I found layer upon layer of confusion: so many opinions from different sources, many of them overcomplicating the fundamental human experience. This is because it's hard to define a feeling in words. Feelings cannot be experienced or truly understood by the rational mind. To try and **explain** feelings using the mind means you're not **experiencing** them using the heart and body. Once you've felt a feeling, then and only then can you use the mind to interpret it as a concept.

Feel in the heart first, then the mind second.

Feelings and emotions

Confusing feelings with emotions is common, as the two are closely linked. Emotions are easier to connect to – especially if you're a woman who struggles with PMT and hormones. At certain times of the month emotions might feel like a tornado letting rip inside you.

Emotions are "energy in motion". An emotion is an energetic response to a thought in the mind. An emotion occurs after the mind has processed a feeling. It then releases a thought, plus a chemical reaction (such as the hormones that are released in times of stress) or an emotion into the body. Imagine an emotion as an after-thought experience. A feeling is felt before an emotion is experienced.

Here's an example. Walking along the street, you spot an ex-boyfriend. Immediately you feel sadness; this is felt before your mind processes the scenario. The break-up was messy, and seeing him reminds you of this. In the moment, you're also reminded of other break-ups and perhaps memories of your parents' divorce. Your mind then processes the experience, releases a negative thought and a painful emotional reaction of anger (because of the way you were treated) or frustration (because you feel powerless). The emotion will move through and out of your body as energy does, but the feeling of sadness will last longer.

Do you ever have a feeling about something, an insight that something might happen – and then it happens? Ever hear a friend say "I have a funny feeling about that"?

Our gut feelings are guiding us in every moment. We're always receiving messages from our intuition: wobbles, butter-flies, tightness or churning alongside a feeling something isn't quite right. At such times we're being divinely guided by our inner radar, and it's telling us to avoid certain situations and go ahead with others. We tend to ignore this guidance, though, if it doesn't match what we see as our needs. So we continue down the path we want to go down, without listening. And then something messes up. We pick ourselves up, dust ourselves down and learn from it.

Imagine if we followed our feelings more. Perhaps it would lead us to new opportunities. We'd grow faster, have more power, more confidence, and experience a much richer life. As great as this sounds, we are all afraid of our power and our ability to be bigger, bolder and more visible so we've become very good at ignoring our intuitive feelings.

The Tools in this chapter are designed to help you feel your feelings again. Are you ready for that? Or do you still feel disconnected or blocked?

Something that often stands in the way of feeling is our attachment to needing to feel. Whenever we need something, we become attached to it. We believe that we're less human if we don't experience it. The attachment makes us believe it's very important for us to experience it. And we'll push it to happen because we believe we need it. As soon as you **need** something, you become dependent on it, or obsessed with having it. You create negative energy around the situation, and it won't feel good to you. You put pressure on yourself and your mind gets hooked on it, which makes it harder. If you need to feel, you'll create expectation and resistance around the experience and it'll be harder to feel, as opposed to feeling easily.

Some people are natural "feelers", while others are organised "thinkers". The tendency towards each is created by the way we've been raised, our genetic information and what we've experienced in our lives. You can be both, but in my experience one will dominate. I am more of a feeler than a thinker.

Tools to help you feel your feelings:

1. HOW DO YOU FEEL? Practise asking yourself the question "How do I feel?" every morning and at other moments during the day. Notice what you feel in your body. Do you feel tightness or tension, heaviness or pain? Acknowledge how you feel out loud. Start this conversation with your body, and create a relationship between you. The simple intention that you want to know how you're feeling, and having curiosity about what's happening with you, is enough to deepen the dialogue.

2. HOW DO YOU WANT TO FEEL? After you've asked yourself how you feel, ask yourself: how do I want to feel? Pay attention to the words that come when you ask yourself. You might hear: supported, loved, safe. Whatever you want to feel, choose to feel it now. Sit with the feeling of "loved", for example, and allow it to fill up your heart and body, until you really relate to that feeling and can feel it in your body. Check back in with the feeling you want to feel. Are you still tuned into that feeling? How can you feel that feeling in every moment, no matter what life throws at you?

3. PROCESS YOUR FEELINGS. Life brings situations that cause you pain. If someone hurts you intentionally, and you immediately feel hurt and pain, it is possible to process your feelings faster and get rid of them.

- Breathe into the place in your body where you feel the pain.
- Imagine that you're sucking the energy of the reaction or pain up into your chest and nose.
- Breathe it out.
- Repeat this exercise and keep doing it until you feel clearer.

CHAPTER

21

How to Receive

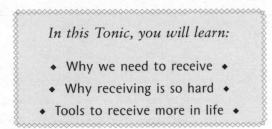

In this Tonic, you will learn:

◆ Why we need to receive ◆

◆ Why receiving is so hard ◆

◆ Tools to receive more in life ◆

Receiving in spiritual terms is the practice of receiving energy into our lives, and it's the key to living an easier, more effortless life. Receiving from the universe is a way of nourishing and replenishing ourselves when we become depleted. It's about drawing in and absorbing the energy flow, as opposed to giving outwards, and moving the energy flow away from us and into something or someone else.

When we receive, we draw in the energy of whatever is available to us in that moment. This could be in the form of material things, such as money and possessions; physical things, such as hugs and neck rubs; or emotional things, such as love and appreciation.

Receiving is much more difficult than we realise. It's much

easier for us to give than receive, because we've been raised to believe this is better for us. Most of us are unable to receive and the result is that we easily become drained and tired. We're not able to restore ourselves emotionally, physically and spiritually and we become frustrated and unhappy. Life is more of a struggle. Our passion and excitement disappear, our life force dims and our spirit weakens.

Energy is freely available to everyone when we learn how to be open and invite it in. We all deserve to receive. Without receiving, we will only achieve a fraction of what we're capable of achieving.

- We need to learn to receive so we can flourish, and become the powerful beings we were born to be.
- We need to be able to receive to restore our health and energy.
- We need to be able to receive so we can be supported in all areas of our lives.
- We need to be able to receive so we can manifest miracles and magic!

Why it's hard to receive

What do you do when someone gives you a compliment?

a) Avoid eye contact, look away, blush and change the subject.
b) Shut down and close inwards.
c) Make eye contact, smile and say thank you.

Most of us would do a) and some even do b) because we find it hard to receive. I'm speaking for the majority of us, so you're not alone.

At some point when we were children, we learned that love could be taken away from us unless we did something in return for it. Now when someone offers us love in any form, we fall into a state of panic and feel vulnerable because the mind raises the alarm. It tells us not to receive because if we do, the love could be withdrawn and taken away at any time. We remember it happening before, we remember the pain and we don't want it to happen again, so we turn it away and shut down. Or we keep our guard so far up we don't even realise love has been offered in the first place.

Many of us have issues around trusting the source or giver of support or love. These aren't necessarily about the person standing in front of us in the moment; they can be about the person who stood in front of us as a child. And it doesn't mean that person was intentionally withholding love; they were simply doing what they believed was the right thing to do at the time.

We've also learned that it's weak to receive, or that if we receive we've failed in some way. Many of us have learned to survive as independent beings, without the support of other people. Perhaps our parents struggled on alone, and we've learned this is the way to be successful in life. But if we carry on in this way, we are missing out on so much that life has to offer.

When we're in receiving mode we draw in more support from our spiritual source, or the universe. When we learn how to receive universal support we'll shift fast, because we have more power or fuel to invest in our inner fire, which keeps us growing and burning brightly.

Receiving support after a lifelong drought is like breathing new, fresh, highly oxygenated air into our lungs, and we suddenly feel alive and free. Life changes and the question isn't "How do I do this?" – it's "When can I do this?" New possibilities suddenly appear in our paths and an abundant stream of offerings flows into our laps.

Receiving is when life really begins. When I learned how to receive, everything shifted up a gear. I couldn't quite believe what was happening on a daily basis. It was astounding – and I want this to happen for you too.

Tools to receive more in your life:

1. PRACTISE RECEIVING GIFTS. When someone gives you a gift or compliment, have the intention to receive the energy and love behind it. Look at the person who is giving you the gift, consciously take the gift in your hands and receive all the love and thought behind it. Even if you don't think much thought and effort went into the choosing, the intention alone to give you a gift is a sign of love. Receive the love behind the gift.

2. RECEIVE THE ENERGY INTO YOUR BODY. Imagine breathing in the energy of whatever is coming your way. If you receive a hug, imagine receiving the energy of the hug right through your body and into your cells. If you receive a compliment, imagine receiving the energy of the words and the love behind them right through your body and into your cells. Dissolve your own barriers to allow love in.

3. RECEIVE YOURSELF. The fastest way to receive is to learn how to receive from yourself. A mirror is the best way to do this. Take your mirror and connect to yourself eye-to-eye. Look yourself in the eyes and tell yourself: "You are amazing. You look great! I support you, I believe in you." Observe any resistance in your body, or any part of you that tenses up, or any thoughts you have that tell you not to do this. It may feel uncomfortable or cheesy or whatever else you tell yourself. This is a practice so you'll need to keep doing it. Face the fear and do it anyway!

CHAPTER

—⟨22⟩—

Stay Zen While Spinning Plates

In this Tonic, you will learn:

- ◆ About our busy addiction ◆
- ◆ To get clear about how busy you are ◆
- ◆ Tools to stay balanced and zen ◆

We're busy bees. We swarm around in our buzzing, fast-paced world. We fly from one activity to the next without taking the time to pause, be present and connect to ourselves.

We're the generation of jugglers, all of us spinning lots of plates at the same time. We're the digital pioneers who can start up a business in a day because it's easier than ever before to create a business and life that we love. We're overflowing with ideas. There's more choice than ever, and more incentive to follow our passion and launch it into cyberspace.

We've learned ways to keep going when we're tired yet still have deadlines to meet. We shift into a hyperactive state because of the coffee we drink, or the adrenaline we're running on, or the energy drinks we glug to fuel us up. We exercise more, eat sugary foods to give us energy and instant meals to save us time. Medicating ourselves is normal practice when the going gets too tough.

———

We're addicted to being busy, reluctant to slow down, addicted to the rush.

———

When friends ask how you are, your default response is, "I'm OK, I'm just really busy!" Sound familiar? We love telling people how busy we are. It makes us feel worthy and important. Why? Because there's a part in us all that believes we're not good enough. We feel inferior and inadequate, and in our own minds whatever we do won't be quite enough. So when we're in a busy cycle, we can immediately feel a sense of worthiness, even though it's false gratification. Immersing ourselves in our work is a way of trying to fill the unworthiness void. It's a great way to escape ourselves and our issues.

Getting stuck in the busy cycle is addictive. Once we create the belief that we're always busy, it becomes an ingrained habit. As we attract more and more things to do, our plate gets heavier and heavier and we become busier and busier.

Our world supports the busyness; at times it feels like the whole universe is speeding up. We're more connected than ever, and our minds are drowning in content. Every minute, Facebook users share 2.5 million posts, and Instagrammers upload almost 220,000 photos. We sleep with our phones under our pillows and check our work emails at 3am. We're plugged in, switched on and tuned in 24/7.

And we show no signs of slowing down anytime soon.

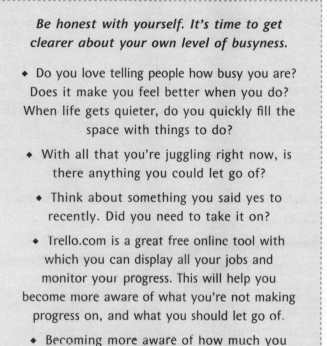

Be honest with yourself. It's time to get clearer about your own level of busyness.

♦ Do you love telling people how busy you are? Does it make you feel better when you do? When life gets quieter, do you quickly fill the space with things to do?

♦ With all that you're juggling right now, is there anything you could let go of?

♦ Think about something you said yes to recently. Did you need to take it on?

♦ Trello.com is a great free online tool with which you can display all your jobs and monitor your progress. This will help you become more aware of what you're not making progress on, and what you should let go of.

♦ Becoming more aware of how much you have on your plate is a good first step.

We're turning into machines

We aren't machines, but we act as if we are. Working non-stop for twelve- or fourteen-hour days without regular breaks, or time outside in the fresh air, or a rest at lunch to energise our minds.

It isn't healthy to work the way we do now. We need to dedicate space and time for our own self-care.

Imagine us as human batteries, losing energy and draining power throughout the day. Come the evening we're completely flat, running only on adrenaline and the double cappuccino we dashed out for at 4pm. We're now tired-but-wired, and this is how we usually get through the day.

Because we only have a finite amount of energy to power us through, we need to be able to recharge our batteries to keep our power flowing. In this way we'll feel good at the end of the day.

What do you do in your lunch hour?

a) I don't take one. Just sit at my desk munching as I work.
b) I reclaim my lunch hour and do a yoga class/ swim/go for a walk.

Can you make the conscious effort to try b)? Invest in yourself by doing something that supports your wellbeing and nourishes your system. If you can't escape from the office/place of work, find somewhere quiet to do a guided meditation; or choose a book (check out the recommended reading on pages 260–1) and read a few chapters.

Do something positive that moves you away from your desk for the hour. You are entitled to this time. You deserve it, and you need it.

Stop saying yes

We say yes to networking events, new opportunities, new jobs, drinks after work, weekends away in the country, having babies, a new puppy, writing our memoirs and so forth. We juggle all of this as well as our day-to-day obligations: admin, emails, meetings, bookings, Instagram, Facebook, caring for our children or elderly parents, checking in with friends. With all the excitement, temptation and FOMO (Fear Of Missing Out), we're quickly in way over our heads and struggling to stay afloat. We tell ourselves: "It's all good, I've got one shot at this", "There's only one life" and "I've got this. I'll sleep when I'm dead."

Life becomes a pressure cooker . . . one more thing, and our heads will blow off. Kerpow!

Stop saying yes! Become aware of how you're saying yes, and track how many times. What are you mostly saying yes to?

We've been taught to believe it's much better to say yes, and agree with everything that's being asked of us. So we happily go along with it all. Some of us do everything we can to make other people happy, and saying yes and meeting everyone's demands and expectations is the aim.

Learning to say no is a crucial skill that we will explore further in Chapter 25 (see page 203).

Tools to stay zen:

1. EMPTY THE BUSY BRAIN. Journalling is a lovely, cleansing process and a good way to empty your mind. Do this every morning and/or evening to release the mountain of tasks in your mind. Invest in a nice notebook of whichever size works for you – I like A4 and plain (not lined) so I have lots of space to write. It's important to let yourself free-flow and write whatever it is on your mind, without correcting yourself or judging what you've written. Let yourself express whatever is waiting to come out: emotions, thoughts about the day you've had or how well you slept. Aim to write at least one side; you might write two. You don't need to re-write or read back what you've written; you might even want to burn it! Do whatever you feel is right.

2. OXYGEN SHOT. Make a fist and tap gently onto the V bone at the top centre of the collarbone, while taking some big, deep breaths. Do this for two or three minutes as you focus on the air going right down and expanding your belly. The tapping action will help you to draw the air into your lungs with less resistance. As soon as more oxygen reaches your bloodstream, you'll feel instantly calmer and clearer.

3. TAP AWAY THE OVERWHELMING FEELINGS. How overwhelmed do you feel right now on a scale of 0 to 10, with 10 being the most overwhelmed? Take your notepad and make some notes about how you feel about your load: for example, "I'm feeling completely overloaded and I can't think straight", "I don't know how to get through all I have on", "No one else understands. I have to do this all on my own." Use the phrases you chose to repeat, while you do a tapping exercise, or follow the ones I've listed below.

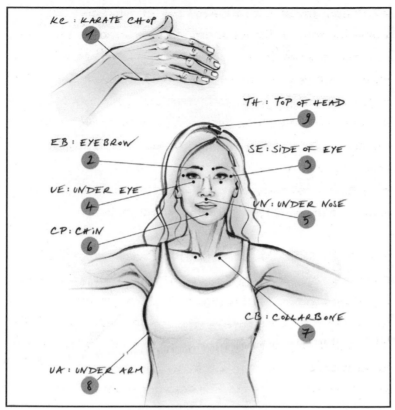

Diagram of tapping points

Practise tapping gently with the first three fingers (index, middle and ring fingers) of one hand on the outside edge of the other hand, the karate-chop point. This is where we begin the tapping sequence.

Karate-chop point: "Even though I'm feeling overwhelmed right now, I deeply and completely accept who I am and how I feel." (Repeat three times.)

Eyebrow point: "I'm completely overloaded . . ."

Side of the eye: . . . and I can't think straight."

Under the eye: "There's too much going on."

Top lip: "I don't know how to get through everything."

Chin: "No one else understands."

Collarbone: "It all feels so hopeless."

Underarm: "There's too much going on right now."

Top of the head: "I'm completely overloaded."

Do a couple of rounds of these shorter phrases until you feel better then move on to this:

Eyebrow point: "I'm willing to surrender."

Side of the eye: "Holding on doesn't serve me."

Under the eye: "There has to be another way."

Top lip: "I'm willing to be open to a solution."

Chin: "I choose to surrender now."

Collarbone: "There has to be another way."

Underarm: "I choose to relax now . . ."

Top of the head: ". . . and know I'm a good person."

Do a couple of rounds of this until you feel more positive.

To finish, take some nice, deep breaths in and thank yourself for letting all this go, and giving in.

Be Less Anxious

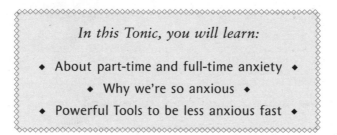

In this Tonic, you will learn:

◆ About part-time and full-time anxiety ◆
◆ Why we're so anxious ◆
◆ Powerful Tools to be less anxious fast ◆

Note: whether you suffer from anxiety full-time or are just a part-time worrier, this chapter is worth a read and the Tools are ace.

When's the last time you felt anxious?

Often it's hard to tell, as we're so used to it being a part of who we are. The symptoms come on suddenly and can quickly become overpowering.

- The mind races so it's hard to think straight.
- The chest feels tight and tense so it's hard to breathe properly.
- The heart flutters, aches and closes down.
- The tummy twists and contorts so it's hard to eat anything.
- The palms sweat and it's easy to lose your grip.
- The mouth dries so that nothing quenches your thirst.

It can feel as if you're losing control of your life and everything's slipping away. As the symptoms intensify, you begin to hyperventilate and/or forget to breathe. In that moment you're frozen with fear and locked inside your negative mind.

Anxiety feels like a little devil that sits on your shoulder waiting for the right moment. It whispers in your ear and waits for you to freak out so it can step in and take over.

For some of us anxiety is ever-present. It's a fact of life, waiting behind the scenes to take us down.

For most of us it's not there all the time, but comes on when we have a deadline, a presentation or something challenging to do. Intense dreams during the night can make us wake up in an anxious mood. There are many triggers that can send us into a spin. Sometimes we feel anxious, and when we analyse it we realise we've no idea why.

Is your mum a massive worrier? Is your dad easily anxious? You can inherit anxiety through your DNA and genetic information, which can activate itself at any time in your life, mostly when you're in an environment that supports the activation – for example, a stressful job. Or equally you can inherit anxiety by growing up with an anxious parent and learning the way they respond to the world, then copying it.

So why are we anxious?

Anxiety is a response to fear. So far, we've picked up lots of reasons to believe that life can be one big nightmare, full of unease, doubt and outright panic. We carry a big bag of worries around with us. We live in fear, and it takes only the tiniest trigger to set us off. If we continue this way our brain goes into overdrive and eventually short-circuits.

We're hard-wired to react to stress and fear in our outside world. We've been doing it since we were hunter-gatherers and running away from tigers and wild beasts. When we were in danger back then, the body released adrenaline and cortisol (the stress hormones) to get energy to our muscles so we could run away. Running burned off the stress hormones, then afterwards we'd rest, recover and get on with our lives.

And now that we don't have to run for our lives? It's the urban jungle we live in fear of. The stress reaction is activated each time we have a fear-based thought. Since we're living in almost constant fear, we keep producing cortisol and adrenaline and feeling more and more anxious. When we feel anxious, we feel fear again and we release more stress hormones. It's a vicious cycle that's hard to break. The faster you become aware of all this, the faster you'll heal.

Anxiety is a part of our lives.

The way we live, especially in cities, actively fuels our worried minds and incessant negative thought patterns.

Some degree of worry is useful in modern life, because it reminds us to take our PowerPoint presentation to the conference, or to work out a way to calm the boss even though it's been impossible to reach the target he set. But next time you find yourself dwelling on a worry, ask yourself what's really going on.

For me, I've found that I get anxious before something I know will mean me facing a fear: for example, negotiating on costs (I hate doing this) or being more visible in some way, perhaps giving a talk to a big crowd. Once I understand what triggers my anxiety, I know why it's coming up, then I can face it head on and see it for what it is: a way of warning me that something's coming that could potentially be dangerous to my wellbeing. Of course in reality it won't be literally dangerous, but my mind thinks it will be.

I recently realised I was mistaking excitement for anxiety. The butterflies in my tummy are confusing. Check in with yourself: are you anxious, or excited – or both?

If this all seems like a lot to take in, and you're feeling more anxious than you did before you read this chapter, relax. And breathe.

Tools to help you be less anxious:

1. TAPPING ON FEELING ANXIOUS. Tapping is a very effective tool for coping with anxiety. Before you tap, take out your notepad and make some notes about how your anxiety makes you feel: for example, "thoughts are out of control, mind is racing, feeling out of place". You can either use these specific phrases as tapping targets or use the ones I've suggested below.

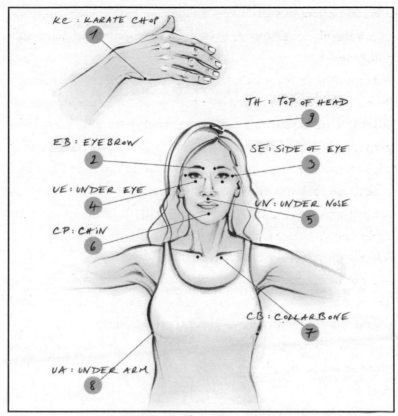

Diagram of tapping points

Ask yourself how anxious you are on a scale of 0 to 10, with 10 being the most anxious.

Tap with the first three fingers (index, middle and ring fingers) of one hand onto the outside edge of the other hand, the karate-chop point. Repeat the phrases below out loud while tapping on the specific points.

Karate-chop point: "Even though I'm feeling very anxious right now, I deeply and completely accept who I am and how I feel." (Repeat three times.)

Eyebrow point: "I'm so anxious right now . . ."

Side of the eye: ". . . and I can't think straight."

Under the eye: "My mind is racing."

Top lip: "I'm so self-conscious."

Chin: "I'm feeling so uncomfortable."

Collarbone: "My thoughts are out of control."

Underarm: "There's too much going on in my mind."

Top of the head: "I just can't think straight."

Do a couple of rounds of these shorter phrases until you feel calmer, and then move on to the below:

Eyebrow point: "I'm willing to surrender."

Side of the eye: "Worrying doesn't serve me."

Under the eye: "There has to be another way."

Top lip: "I'm willing to surrender."

Chin: "I choose to surrender now."

Collarbone: "There has to be another way."

Underarm: "I choose to relax now."

Top of the head: "And know I'm a good person."

Do a couple of rounds of this, until you feel more positive.

To finish, take some nice, deep breaths in and thank yourself for calming yourself down.

2. EMPTY THE FEAR BIN. Fears can only control you when they're hidden. Once you name your fears, they become less powerful. So if you're feeling anxious and it's getting more intense, it can help to list your fears out loud. I watched a video of author Sonia Choquette empty the fear bin with a presenter and it make so much sense. Do this with your partner or a friend you trust. Arrange for them to be on call, either by phone, Skype or in person. Explain that you want to empty your "fear bin", and you need their help to coax everything out of you. Begin by listing all that you feel afraid of. Your fears might sound like this: "I'm afraid I'm going to fail", "I'm afraid of making a mistake", "I'm afraid of getting it wrong". Ask whoever is helping you to interject gently and keep asking "What else?" when they feel you closing up or running out of steam. Listing all your fears and bringing them into the light of day will take the power away from them.

3. PARTY WITH IT. Invite your anxiety to come out and party with you. Sit somewhere quiet – it could be on a toilet seat if you're at work. Close your eyes and take some nice, deep breaths into your body. Notice where you feel the anxiety in your body. Is it in your stomach, or heart or chest? Sit with it, breathe into it and invite it to be here more strongly. That might sound like a crazy idea but the more you invite the anxiety to be present, the less it will be. Anxiety sits in the wings, whispering into your ear. It doesn't like being in the light with you, so it waits until you are worried, negative and weak, and makes a move. Don't wait until then; invite it to be fully here and present with you now. If it's going to ruin your life, it may as well do so in style and be brave enough to come out and face you (of course, it won't).

4. DAILY MEDITATION IS MEDICATION. A morning meditation will make you instantly feel more balanced, centred and strong in yourself. You'll find a selection to try on my website.

Letting Go

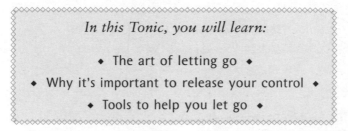

In this Tonic, you will learn:

◆ The art of letting go ◆

◆ Why it's important to release your control ◆

◆ Tools to help you let go ◆

Are you a control *freeeeaak*?

If things don't go to plan, does it make you twitchy?

This isn't just your story; most of us cling on tightly to our lives and everything in it. We're desperate not to give up control or drop anything we're juggling.

Physically, we're holding on. Our insides are rigid. We're tight in our hips, our shoulders, our chests, our digestive systems. We're terrified of being prised open. Only occasionally do we reveal a crack, letting others see the beauty inside, like an oyster showing a glimpse of its pearl.

The more we cling on, the more we suffer from inner pain, which affects our overall health and happiness. We use up masses of energy to hold us in, and keep us closed and controlled.

As a society we are clinging onto old stories, old patterns, old behaviours, old relationships, old friendships, old jobs. We keep getting ourselves stuck, and resist anyone who attempts to change us. We believe we're safer holding on, but ultimately we're not. The walls or foundations of old structures can come crashing down on us at any time. There's only so much pain we can take before something has to give.

There is another way. It's called letting go.

If this sounds glaringly obvious – it is. But as easy as it might sound to do – it isn't.

Letting go is an art. It takes practice and commitment to make progress. It is one of the most challenging things you can do in life. But don't let that put you off. The practice of letting go, no matter what level you're on, will help you in some way. Even if it takes a while to understand. View it as a long-term investment, and an ongoing work in progress.

I have some Tools to help speed up your process, but the commitment to practice has to come from you.

The benefits of letting go

Letting go of everything you're trying to control is vital to living a fuller, richer life. Here's why:

- We all crave the feeling of freedom, and letting go gives us freedom. We set ourselves free of our worries, stress, suffering and pain.
- We release attachments to plans, which opens up space for more spontaneity and surprises. Better things than we ever imagined will be possible.
- Our health and energetic systems are regulated and supported to flow naturally and restore themselves, increasing our levels of wellbeing.
- Letting go moves us into the present moment, allowing us to enjoy and cherish our lives in the now.
- Ultimately, we will be happier. We're in our natural state when we are not worrying about retaining control.

Life is full of "surprises". It springs them on us all the time. The laptop crashes with all our work on it, we lose our phone containing our personal photos, our train breaks down on our way to work, or that date we'd been excited about cancels at the last minute. We can be tripped up at any time by events that are completely out of our control. Life (or the majority of it) is out of our control. We think we're in control, but we're not.

We can't control the train to make sure it's not late, we can't control our immune system to protect ourselves from getting ill, we can't control our hard drives to stop them from crashing. We can't control other people, no matter how hard we try.

We simply don't have control of what happens in our outside world. Most of us fall into the trap of needing to be in control. It's a trap because we're under the illusion that we can be in control, we can't.

The problem is that our minds love certainty. Our ideal dream scenario is to feel safe and secure in our own skin, to know where we're headed and what to expect in every moment. We want complete control over every aspect of our lives. We want to know our destiny and to understand our universe. We crave the reassurance of knowing that we are in the driving seat. We become attached to outcomes, and try to manipulate things to happen the way we want them to. We picture the ideal scenario in our minds and when it doesn't happen according to plan, we push and push and create more resistance. We feel angry and frustrated which makes it all worse. It's a vicious cycle.

And if you relate to this, I want you to take a couple of deep breaths right now, and ask yourself to be open to hearing me out. I'll use the ripping off the plaster analogy again: it might hurt a little at first and then it'll feel OK. Read the next paragraph a few times and see how you go.

———

We have NO control of our outside world. The idea that we have control is an illusion created by our minds to keep us safe and protected. Things will happen to us every single day that are completely beyond our control. What makes us feel anxious is when we try to grab hold of these situations and force them to happen in a certain way. As we try our hardest to control all aspects of our lives, we only create more fear and anxiety in the process.

———

Take a nice, deep breath now. And release.

It's really positive to come to terms with the reality that you're not in control. Your life will change when you do.

So let go, and do it now. The longer you wait, the more you'll miss.

Tools to help you let go:

1. **"I LET GO, I SURRENDER, I GIVE IN."** Say these mantras out loud whenever you need help to let go. Direct them to anywhere in your body you feel as if you're holding on, and they will help you to release. You're giving yourself an instruction to follow. The intention to say these phrases creates an energetic response and space in your mind and body. Your higher self listens, feels the space and knows you've asked for intervention and help.

2. **GIVE IT UP.** Whatever you're trying to control, offer it up to the universe for assistance. Simply say to the universe: "Thank you for helping me let this go, thank you for taking this from me, thank you for your assistance." Say this daily until you feel clearer. Know that it's gone to a higher place, and will be transformed in the best way. Perhaps a solution will come up, perhaps not, but at least you know it's been dealt with in the best way for all concerned.

3. **FLOATING.** Do this in your bed. Move away all pillows, cushions and blankets so you have a flat surface. Lie down on your bed, on your back, and close your eyes. Tell yourself: "I let

go, I let go." Repeat this gently over and over until you feel totally relaxed. Notice how your body feels as if you're floating in water or suspended in animation. If you fall asleep, that's fine; it's a practice and I know you'll find it very restorative. Enjoy!

4. **LOVE YOUR NEEDINESS.** Do this while meditating or simply sitting somewhere quietly. Close your eyes. Your intention is to connect to the needy parts of yourself that you are holding onto. You're trying to control and hold on for a reason. You either need to feel loved, or need attention or kindness. Be understanding of yourself, and send love to the parts of you that are needy. When they feel the love, they'll more easily let go.

5. **PRACTISE PRESENCE.** It's easy to miss what's happening right now in this moment. We're locked into either the future, worrying about what's going to happen, or the past, obsessing over what's already happened. When we're like this, we miss the life unfolding before our eyes.

- Inhale deeply into your body and hold it for seven counts, then release it and exhale. Repeat this another six times, so you do it seven times in total.
- Become more aware of your surroundings. Take a few moments to look around at where you are. Notice every little detail, from the textures of the fabrics around you, to the smells, sounds, colours and all the objects in your awareness. Don't do anything else except drink in your surroundings. Do this very slowly for five minutes.

Saying No

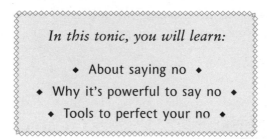

In this tonic, you will learn:

♦ About saying no ♦
♦ Why it's powerful to say no ♦
♦ Tools to perfect your no ♦

It isn't easy to say no.

In fact, the very thought of it makes me wince. I'm not very good at saying no.

How do you feel about saying no? Be honest with yourself.

If someone says no to you, how does it make you feel? It's not very nice, is it? Actually, it feels as if you're being punished for something. From an early age, we're pre-programmed with the belief that it's much better that we say yes and go along with whatever Mummy/Daddy/teacher/babysitter wants us to do. "No" isn't a word we should use. It's bad to say no; no means trouble ahead.

When we say yes and are good, we get a treat, a reward and love.

When we say no and are naughty, we get punished, rejected or ignored.

It doesn't feel good to say no, does it? I'd much rather say yes and get positive, good things, as opposed to being sent to the naughty corner for doing the opposite.

But yes isn't always the best way.

Saying yes too often is an easy way of burning ourselves out, and giving too much of ourselves to others.

We might be doing good for others, but we are completely ignoring our own needs.

Saying yes to everything is the fastest way to drain our power, and deplete our energy in different ways:

- Physically and mentally: running around from event to event, fulfilling other people's plans, having too many things to think about, and no time to rest and recharge.
- Spiritually and energetically: resistance from pushing against the natural flow of life, ignoring our spiritual guidance and using lots of energy to make things happen.

If your diary heaves with plans for other people and no time for yourself, it's easy to get overwhelmed. This is a major problem. When we don't take care of ourselves, we can fall apart at the cost of pleasing others. And it's not only our loved ones who suffer; we suffer too. When this happens, achieving the life we desire becomes an unrealistic dream.

We need to take back the power of saying no.

Why saying no is more loving than saying yes

If you go along with something because you're afraid to say no, you are not giving the other person enough credit. As I explained in Chapter 8, they will sense your lack of clarity and commitment, and feel an underlying resentment or negativity towards you. Even if they might not obviously react, they may feel it subconsciously.

When you say yes because you're afraid to say no, the yes comes from a place of fear and not because you are being loving towards the other person. In that moment you are not loving them or giving them the most truthful version of yourself.

Saying no is your most loving response, and one that is the most authentic coming from you. Even if it means they express disappointment because you aren't able to be a part of their plan, they will accept your no and understand it at some level.

Too much of our time is spent worrying about what others think of us. If we didn't care, saying no would be so much easier. The fact is, we have no control over other people's opinions and thoughts. There is no way to influence them; they will react based on their own belief systems and the programming they received in their childhoods. They might judge us, reject us or criticise us and there is absolutely nothing we can do about it.

Coming to terms with this is an important step forwards to reclaiming your life and maintaining your energy.

There's a deep fear of missing out, and that if we say "no" our friends will forget or reject us. As many of us have old rejection wounds already, we don't want to risk upsetting or losing anyone we're close to.

Most of us feel the fear each time we think about saying no. For some people this is so great that the word is wiped from their vocabulary. They say yes straight away, before they even venture towards a possible no.

As humans we're highly skilled in diversionary techniques – anything to avoid facing ourselves and the pain we're hiding underneath. The busiest people in the world are the ones who are running away from themselves the most. You can be sure they have some deep wounds they're avoiding facing. Saying yes to yet another event gives them another excuse not to spend time with themselves.

Saying yes to people when we actually want to say no affects our self-confidence and lowers our self-esteem. We lose trust in ourselves, and our ability to make intuitive decisions. We are not honouring the truth of what we feel. We are not listening to our own wisdom and acting on it. Instead, we're saying yes from a place of fear.

The trick is to learn how to read situations intuitively and make decisions according to our intuition. How does it feel if you think about saying yes? If you feel your body closing and tensing up, this isn't serving you. Imagine if you said no: how would your body feel? If you sense your body opening and expanding, it's better for you to say no this time. Practise responding according to your intuition and you will be reacting from a place of honesty that your family, friends and colleagues will respect.

Tools to help you say no:

1. BE HONEST. Grow some balls. Say no, and tell the person concerned exactly why. Tell them you don't like going to museums, or you don't enjoy getting hammered any more, or you feel socially anxious around that particular group of friends. Whoever is on the receiving end will admire you much more for being honest.

2. PRACTISE SAYING NO. Use a mirror to help support you with this. Pick an event or a request you have to respond to, and practise talking to the person concerned, telling them why you are not able to attend. Be honest and let them know that you're very grateful for the invitation, but that you need a rest and time to recharge.

3. NO FROM THE HEART. Speaking from the heart raises the energy and vibration of the whole conversation. When you speak from your heart, you are speaking from your most authentic self and people will receive it as such. You cannot lie from your heart. Tell them no, and tell them why. Be honest and let them know that they are amazing to spend time with but that you need the time for yourself right now. You'll feel empowered when you walk away. They will feel loved, even though you're saying no.

Clear the Drains

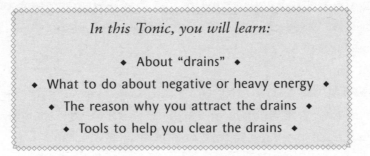

In this Tonic, you will learn:

♦ About "drains" ♦

♦ What to do about negative or heavy energy ♦

♦ The reason why you attract the drains ♦

♦ Tools to help you clear the drains ♦

A drain is someone you sense is heavy-going. Their energy is draining and you feel as if it saps yours. The thought of being around them fills you with resistance, and you do your absolute best to avoid spending time with them. They drain your energy and suck you dry. You tell yourself they have bad energy, lots of issues and should be swerved at all costs.

Except they keep calling. They like meeting up with you. They're dying to see you and keep telling you, "We have so much to catch up on".

So you go for dinner after work. You keep them happy.

An hour into your evening together, you feel as if you've been up for three days with no sleep, and are completely and utterly zonked and running on empty. When you get home, you can't even talk or do anything except fall into bed and sleep until morning.

Why does this keep happening? Annoyed at yourself, once again you make a mental note not to see them any more.

This is a dilemma we often find ourselves in. Do particular people spring to mind as you're reading this? Are there certain friends, or colleagues or even family members who fit the bill?

Take out your notebook now, and make a list of people in your life who are drains.

♦ *Remember:* this list is only for you. You're not a bad person for making it. I give you permission. It's for the sake of your sanity, energy and wellbeing. It'll become clear soon enough.

♦ Next to each person, write down the qualities which annoy you about them. Is it that they're tight with money, or they gossip about others?

♦ Be honest as you do this exercise. We're going to try to understand why this happens, and what to do about it later on. For now, it's important you get clear on who this applies to.

Why does it happen?

Imagine everyone in your life as a mirror, reflecting back different aspects of yourself – some of which you don't want to own up to. You can call these your "shadows". On paper, these shadows do not make you look very good. In fact, if you read out your list of shadows you would sound like a terrible person. We try to avoid examining our shadows at all costs, preferring to live in complete denial that they exist. We wouldn't want anyone to think we were negative people. The idea of having shadows makes us feel really uncomfortable.

But these shadows exist whether you deny it or not. And because of this, you'll be sending out information to the universe from your shadows and be receiving people who match your shadow resonance into your space. And because your beautiful soul wants you to heal, your intuition will also be guiding you towards the perfect opportunities for healing to take place. All you need do is accept this is the case, and recognise the healing opportunity.

This is where we usually fall down, because we don't understand that the "drain" sitting in front of us provides the perfect healing opportunity for us. The reason we feel so drained is because when we're seeing ourselves in their mirror, we're connecting with our shadows. Since we are unwilling to face them, our brain is sending us signals to "avoid" in an effort to keep us protected and shut down.

What can we do about it?

From where I'm sitting, there are two clear options:

- **Escape and run the other way.** Make excuses and leave. You don't want to spend time with anyone who makes you feel low on energy. These people will suck your energy dry. Best to get outta there, and fast.

◆ **Stick around and grow.** Think about the mirror idea. Maybe what annoys you about them is a quality that you possess (or used to possess) as well. Why do they drain you? What is it about them that sucks you dry? What frustrates you about them? Check what you wrote in your list earlier. For example, do they constantly make judgements about other people and situations? Does it pain you to be around them because of their bitching and moaning about others? Now ask yourself: is there a part of you, possibly buried somewhere deep down, who is judgemental too? Were you bitchy and judgemental back in your school days? Was this something you were guilty of, and now you're holding onto the shame that you felt about all the people you judged?

Get the idea?

What if there's a part of you inviting in your friend's negativity and judgements? You have the same parts of your personality, except they're hidden away and you are in complete denial about them. Don't worry, I would be too. No one likes to own up to being a judge!

When we identify the shadows, we get access to big gifts of transformation inside them.

---

to admit to the shadows is the hard part; usually
outside our understanding of who we are as a person.

asy to point the finger at our drains and assume they
are the source of the negative energy that threatens to drain
us. It makes our egos feel good, because it positions them
beneath us in some way. This becomes a cycle, and we'll
happily keep pointing the finger elsewhere to avoid looking
at our own stuff.

You need to start calling yourself out on your avoidance and
owning up to your fibs (even if they are fibs with good intentions). As responsible people, we have to start taking ownership
of ourselves and our own struggles, weaknesses and issues. We
need to make a commitment to transform ourselves from the
inside, rather than pointing the finger to the outside world,
which is our default reaction.

Tools to help you clear the drains and feel good doing it:

1. VISUALISE YOUR DRAIN. Go to your meditation spot.
Close your eyes and take some nice, deep breaths to connect
to your body. Take some time to relax and breathe before you
do anything else. When you're ready, tune into the person
who is a drain and imagine them standing in front of you.
Pay special attention to how your body reacts to them being
there. Sense how you feel around this person without them
being there in person. Do you feel your body tighten? Stay
with it. Sense it, connect with it, then stand back and disen-
gage. Allow it to unravel and move through you, to release.

2. CALL OUT YOUR SHADOW. Use your list of people who drain you, and what annoys you about them, to identify your shadows. If you have a strong reaction or feel very emotional, then it's likely you are concealing your own shadows. Own them now by naming the shadow, e.g. jealousy, admitting it is yours, and slowly repeating it a few times, e.g. I am jealous, until you feel more neutral and less emotional. Go through the entire list of people, identifying their annoying traits and owning each one as yours. You'll soon begin to feel freer.

3. BE IN A COCOON OF LIGHT. When you're sitting with a drain, use this tool to protect your energy. Sit down and close your eyes. Imagine a stream of white light flowing down onto your head like a shower. It moves down your face and body until it surrounds you with healing light. A big oval of white light forms all around you and joins up beneath your feet, as if you are enclosed in an egg shape. Stay with this vision for a few minutes until you can see it is thick in texture. Thank it for protecting and surrounding you.

4. RELEASE NEGATIVE ENERGIES. Use this at any time you feel you've been around negative people, or in negative situations. It's a useful way to reset your energy field. Say this phrase out loud: "Thank you for releasing all negative energies and influences from all levels of my being. Thank you for cleaning my energy field and restoring my power. It is done. Thank you."

CHAPTER

—⟨27⟩—

Make Peace with the Parents

> *In this Tonic, you will learn:*
>
> ◆ How influential your parents are ◆
> ◆ Why blaming your parents isn't helping you ◆
> ◆ Tools to help you restore peace with your parents ◆

What's the story with your parents?

Do you know them or not? Love them or not? Are they still around or passed away?

Whether you realise it or not, there's no denying that your parents played a big part in creating the person you are today.

Do you adore them? Or do they massively get on your nerves? Or both?

If you're under seventeen they probably embarrass you; over 25, they're more useful and your opinions of them are rising.

Your relationship with your parents shifts and changes throughout your life, as you shift and change. Love them or hate them, they're here for the long haul (at least I hope yours are). And believe it or not, most are doing the best that they can, even though at times it doesn't feel like it.

It's fair to say we're all on our own unique parent journey, and it takes time to understand what they mean to you. Because they've known you since birth, you have years' worth of experiences, memories, emotions and feelings between you. They know your most intimate secrets from childhood, and are armed with information that can take you down kicking and screaming. They know your weak spots, and how to exploit them without you even realising. You've been your most vulnerable around them – which is fine if you feel safe, but a problem if you don't.

No matter the circumstances surrounding your birth, your parents created you together, and you were born through them, so you're a part of their gene pool and you share DNA. You have them in you, and you see yourself in them. There is no escaping this fact of life.

You now have two choices: make peace with them and free yourself in the process, or stay at war and suffer.

Our parents are our main teachers

Mum and Dad were the first people who helped to create and shape who you are now. From the moment we're born, we absorb everything in our environment into our sponge-like brains, hearts and cells. Fresh into the world, we are clear, open, primed and ready for information. We're impressionable, mouldable and have no filters, so we soak up everything without knowing what is or isn't good for us.

We absorb our parents' conversations, their behaviours and their experiences. We observe them, their patterns and how they interact with other people, especially our grandparents. We absorb their energies of fear and limitation. We notice the way they relate to us, whether they are confident or anxious as parents, how often they're around (or not) and how they connect with us emotionally.

Imagine all the information you've taken in over the years. Think about what was happening between your parents when you were little. It's good to understand the home environment you were in during those early years.

Think about the following questions:

- Did they argue a lot or split up when you were a child?
- Were they loving with you? Or were they closed and shut down?
- Were they both employed?
- Did they work close by or far away?
- How were they financially? Did they have money worries?

As I explained in Chapter 1, it's common to not remember parts of your childhood, especially if there was any negativity or suffering. The brain blocks out the bad bits. But have a think now, because remembering is the first step towards healing any scars.

Among other lessons we learn from our parents, we learn about relationships. The way our parents related to us in the early years created the foundation for our own values and beliefs and influenced how we now behave in our current relationships. For example, if your mum and dad were emotionally unavailable to you, and didn't always notice or recognise if you needed them, you sensed that absence of emotional connection, attention and love. As a child you might have reacted by doing whatever you could to be noticed. Playing up, sabotaging the games in nursery school, or being very loud and disruptive are all signs of trying to be seen. You might have been told off for being an "attention seeker" when all you wanted was to be loved. Other children might react to a lack of emotional connection with one or both of their parents by withdrawing inside themselves, feeling insecure and unlovable.

As these scars are usually left unhealed, you'll find yourself stuck in playing out behaviours in your adult life. Even if the relationship you're in now is completely different from the one you had with your parents, you could still be subconsciously insecure about your emotional needs being met.

———

Being more aware of how you've been affected by your parents is a very positive move forwards.

———

It helps you to see your relationships in a new light. You'll realise why you behave the way you do, and why you feel so wounded at times. Knowledge gives you the power to do something about it, and begin to change your dynamics. We all desire happiness in our relationships, and this is a way to get it.

Blaming the parents

When you begin to become more aware of your childhood, and see how influenced you were by your parents, a common reaction is to feel resentment. It's easy to blame Mum and Dad for what we see as our faults or weaknesses, especially if your childhood was a traumatic one. It's sometimes easier to blame them than face up to your unhealed wounds, so don't fall into this trap.

When we hold onto blame, we create resistance that blocks us from moving forwards and healing ourselves. It's often not easy to forgive, especially if we're still traumatised or were treated badly by one or both parents. But by holding onto blame and resentment, the only person you are actually hurting is yourself.

Do you want to hurt yourself? Right now, that's exactly what you're doing.

Instead, think about it in another way and use it to your advantage.

Chances are, you're struggling in the same areas your parents were struggling in. So when you look at them, you see your own issues reflected back at you. This can be very painful, especially if you're trying to avoid facing your stuff. You might not realise it yet but if you want an indication of what your issues are, look at what annoys or frustrates you about your parents. The more annoyed you feel, the deeper the issue you are battling. For example, maybe it drives you crazy how anxious your mother is all the time. Her worrying really annoys you. Why can't she just be normal and relaxed?

Now be honest with yourself: is there a part of you that gets anxious? Dig deep, and get real. Sometimes we don't notice our anxiety because it just seems part and parcel of modern life. What types of situations make you feel worried or rattled? Perhaps there's an anxious part of you that you're not aware of yet.

———

Examining what annoys us about our parents can give us a way to heal our own unseen wounds.

———

This works!

Choosing your parents before you're born

Astrologers and many spiritual practitioners believe that we choose our parents before birth. (Bear with me if this sounds a little too wacky for you.)

What if this was the case?

What would be the reason for it?

Imagine life as a kind of university, in which we've pre-decided the topics we want to study before being born. Our souls contain all of our history and the challenges that have arisen in each of our previous lifetimes, including any that we did not finish dealing with. We know on a soul level which topics we need to learn more about so we create a design for the next life, with a forecast and ideas as to how it'll play out in our favour. As we do this, we identify specific souls to invite into our lives who need experience in similar topics to us. We choose them to support us, and together we learn and expand.

These specific souls can be parents, lovers, children, friends and others around us at various points in our lives. They also choose us too.

Too much to take on right now? Don't worry! This isn't for everyone. It's worth staying open to the idea, though, as one day it might give you a new perspective on your dynamic with your parents.

The main thing is learning to accept them as human beings, flaws and all, who want the best for you, even if the way they think you should lead your life does not align with the way you want to live it. This is the path to finding peace with them and moving forwards in yourself.

Tools for finding peace with the parents:

1. LOVE THEM ANYWAY. An easy way to bring more harmony to your relationship is to pinpoint the main thing that drives you mad about them, and learn to love them anyway. Find a quiet spot, close your eyes and breathe in. Visualise one or both of them in front of you. Say to them: "Even though you're . . . [whatever the flaw is], I love you anyway." Repeat this a few times until you feel relieved. In saying this, you are also talking to yourself and the part of you who feels the same way, which also results in you experiencing the relief.

2. GET PERSPECTIVE. A good way to bring more understanding into the dynamic is to do some investigation. What kind of people were their parents (your grandparents)? As a grandchild, your relationship with them will be very different, so ask your parents what they were like as parents. Your parents learned how to behave through your grandparents, so they've inherited their topics from them. Understanding this will help you to understand your parents a bit more.

3. GIVE BACK THE BAGGAGE. If you know you're carrying issues of your parents', such as your mum's depression or your dad's workaholism, you can give back the energy of them. This really works, and will offer some relief, so be open to the possibility of being able to do this. It's likely you'll need further support from a practitioner to go deeper, but this is a great start. Do this in meditation:

- Sit in a quiet place (your sacred space, perhaps), close your eyes and breathe in deeply to relax.
- Move your focus down to your hips and pelvis and connect your awareness with this part of your body.
- Remain here for a while to help you strengthen your connection so you feel more rooted in your body.
- Move your focus to your left side and shoulder. Imagine a seat behind your left shoulder. This is your mother's seat. Invite her into her seat and visualise her sitting down.
- Imagine a parcel on your lap, representing the issue you want to give back to her, and pass it over to her seat slowly. Say to her in your mind, "It's too heavy for me"

and also "Thank you for taking this back". Notice how you feel in your body when doing this. You might want to repeat this a couple of times until you feel like you've given it back, or feel more relieved.

- Move your focus to your right side and shoulder. Imagine a seat behind your right shoulder. This is your father's seat. Invite him into his seat and visualise him sitting down.

- Imagine a parcel on your lap, representing the issue you want to give back to him, and pass it back to his seat slowly. Say to him in your mind, "It's too heavy for me" and also, "Thank you for taking this back". Notice how you feel in your body when doing this. You might want to repeat this a couple of times until you feel like you've given it back, or feel more relieved.

If you don't know your parents (because you were adopted or orphaned at an early age), you can still do this exercise imagining them as columns of light instead. It doesn't matter if you can't fully visualise them; you can still give back to them any baggage you are carrying.

Cure Your Sleep

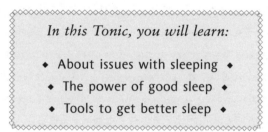

In this Tonic, you will learn:

- ◆ About issues with sleeping ◆
- ◆ The power of good sleep ◆
- ◆ Tools to get better sleep ◆

Sleep is an important aspect of your spiritual and self-care practice. The time and space to regenerate yourself are essential for healing, nourishment and to process all the information and experiences from the day. You need sleep to reset your energy and maintain a high energetic vibration.

We all seem to have our own beliefs about sleep. "I'll sleep when I'm dead!" an ex-boyfriend of mine used to say all the time. I often felt the same way when I was at a party and wrapped up in the moment. Sometimes life is far too exciting to go to sleep; the idea would seem like "giving in".

For those who suffer from insomnia or have night terrors, sleep can come to be seen as challenging and they dread the approach of bedtime.

What are your thoughts about sleep?

- Do you crave eight hours?
- Can you survive on six?
- Do you stay up until 2am watching Netflix?
- Do you crash out at 10pm?

It can be very hard to sleep because of all the stimulation we receive during our daily lives. Our minds are often completely wired for hours after the working day is over. We're still trying to process and sort through a million pieces of information we've been asked to respond to. There's so much to do, and so much we need to figure out, that our brains are still active until the point at which we decide we need to go to sleep. Sometimes this is as little as ten minutes before we get into bed.

Watching TV, listening to podcasts, reading a magazine or whatever else we do before we go to bed keeps our brains active. We need to give our minds the chance to wind down and move into a rest mode, and if we have overactive minds, this can take a while. Expecting to get into bed, for our minds to switch off, and for us to fall into a deep, relaxing sleep, isn't realistic. We aren't designed that way. You might fall asleep easily, but is the quality of sleep you're getting good enough? Do you still feel tired when you wake in the morning? Maybe your brain hasn't had the rest you think it has.

There's no denying sleep is important

Scientists have shown that toxins are cleared out from the brain while we're in deep sleep, so it's a vital part of our cleansing and restoration process. Sleep refreshes the mind, body and heart and restores energy levels. We need sleep to reset our systems and recharge our energy. Do you remember earlier I compared us to batteries? Well, we need to recharge fully.

The first half of a night's sleep restores the body, the second half replenishes the mind. There's no cheat or shortcut to reach that second half. You have to reach it the long way, by going through around four hours of deep sleep where the blood pressure drops, the breathing slows, the muscles relax and your system bathes in restorative hormones. Only then can the mind-replenishing start.

———

Sleep is especially important when you're processing information from the past and healing yourself.

———

It's the opportunity to surrender and allow regeneration to happen naturally.

When we climb into our beds, we're still carrying the resistance, stress, tightness and tension from the day. Our minds, bodies and souls are still living in the experiences and memories we've had. We're still on high alert in case any danger comes our way.

Letting go of this resistance is essential, to enable us to relax and move into a natural and easy flow of sleep. Finding ways to do this, and learn how to wind down before we go to sleep is something we all have to do. Here are my methods.

Tools to get better sleep:

1. MAKE YOUR BEDROOM A PLACE OF RELAXATION AND TRANQUILITY. It should be a place where your intention is to relax and wind down as you move into a restful sleep. Arianna Huffington suggests that when you view your bedroom as a spa, you reframe the energy around sleep and it becomes sacred to you. When your beliefs about sleep improve, so will the quality of your sleep. Invest in some nice bedding and a comfortable mattress and create an abundant place of sacred sleep. Invest well and you'll feel loved and nourished.

2. SLEEP PREPARATION. This is a pre-sleep practice my mum swears by! Think about winding down 30 minutes before you want to go to sleep to give your mind the opportunity, time and space to relax itself. Stop all activities such as emails, TV, social media, listening to the radio. Run a bath with Epsom salts (these help your muscles relax, and detox your system), your choice of delicious-smelling essential oils and scented candles, and soak for 15 to 20 minutes. Afterwards, put on your nightwear, get into bed and relax.

3. REMOVE ALL TECHNOLOGY FROM THE BEDROOM. We are energy so we're sensitive to vibration and static from technology. If you have any technology in the bedroom, your energy system will be interrupted. Switch off the Wi-Fi at night if possible because the static from it can affect your energy. Try it and see if you notice any difference. Don't fall into the habit of keeping your phone by the bedside because you're using it as an alarm. Buy a bedside alarm clock instead.

4. EXPRESS YOUR GRATITUDE. Be grateful for neutral objects that don't hold any emotional charge, such as the comfortable pillow, the mattress, the cosy quilt or luxury blanket you have on your bed. This is important: don't disturb your mindset by dwelling on work, family or your partner before dropping off to sleep in case something negative comes up.

5. MEDITATION FOR DEEPER SLEEP.

- Right before bedtime, get into your bed and sit propped up by a cushion.
- Take some nice, deep breaths in and relax.
- Begin to notice your breathing, and which part of your body you are naturally breathing into.
- Rest your awareness there to give your mind something to focus on.
- Stay there for as long as possible focusing on the sensations, then take a big, deep breath in, and hold it for eight counts before gently releasing.
- Repeat this eight times until you feel calmer.
- Let go of the day's resistance by saying to yourself: "I surrender" and "I let go" and repeating it over and over until you feel relief.

—⟨29⟩—

Get Your Supernatural High

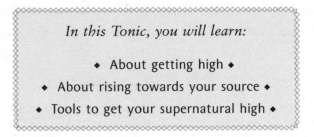

In this Tonic, you will learn:

♦ About getting high ♦

♦ About rising towards your source ♦

♦ Tools to get your supernatural high ♦

We're always craving a fix, a quick boost or a "high".

In Chapter 2, I talked about how some of us use substances such as alcohol and drugs to escape ourselves. However, the "high" I'm talking about in this chapter is different. Our spirits and souls are craving supernatural highs: bliss, euphoria, enlightenment, love and light. Whether we realise it or not, something inside of us longs to feel euphoric.

Is this realistic or just a dream state?

Does this only exist in the minds of spiritual seekers?

In a sense, we're already trying to feel it as we:

♦ drink our morning coffee or an energy drink to
  raise our vibes;

- hit the gym or Barry's Bootcamp for the post work-out buzz;
- fall in love and open ourselves up to another person;
- do a juice cleanse or detox;
- go on a yoga retreat.

Have you ever felt this type of "high"? Think back.

It's pure bliss, like suddenly being catapulted to another universal dimension. In that moment, life feels overwhelmingly perfect and you just want to stay in this bubble forever.

When we're naturally high, we feel joyful, amazing and in love with life. Plus we have a higher ability to manifest (see Chapter 15), and great things will happen. Life goes up a gear.

Our souls and spirits drive us towards our highest state.

Underneath our human skin, bones, tissue and muscles, our pure form is universal energy, love and light.

Imagine us as beings made of bright light; this is who we truly are at our core.

Our bright light is connected to a huge, divine light source and this is where we originally came from. We were born as high-vibrating energetic essences, alive with possibility and excitement. Our "journey" is to return to our essence as much as we can while in our human form. In doing this, we experience the best of the best: euphoria, epic happiness, ecstasy and an inner knowing that everything is perfect. Most importantly, our worries fade away.

Essentially, what this means is reconnecting to our spiritual selves. To do this we have to remove all the blocks standing in our way, and the biggest block is that we are constantly resisting being loved, happy, free, easy and effortless. Makes no sense, I know; but we are more comfortable living in darkness than the light. As humans, we're programmed to suffer and struggle, and we believe life must be hard and challenging for us to succeed. For example, the common belief "I have to work really hard to earn money" means that we'll work ourselves even harder than we need to in order to earn a living. What if we learned to value ourselves properly instead? We could raise our prices, feeling confident that people who value our services would pay a higher fee to receive them, as they'll understand the value we offer.

The good news is that regardless of this, our deepest desire is to be open to the world, receiving all of life and our universe. Our destination is maximum expansion and infinite possibilities. We will get there at some point :-).

The reconnection to your spirit requires commitment and dedication to a spiritual practice, such as meditation or other Tools outlined in this book. You have to find the courage within yourself to make time for your practice. It won't happen without you getting behind it. The more you practise your Tools and clear out the old ways of thinking and being, the more space there is for you to connect to your source and feel the high vibrational essence, energy and light from within you. Commit to your spiritual practice and clearing out the "weeds", and the rest will fall into place.

In the meantime, here are some ways to help you live a more high-vibe, blissful life.

Tools to get your supernatural high:

1. BE MORE GRATEFUL. Consistently expressing gratitude for everything in your life alters your energetic biochemistry because when you're grateful you release endorphins, which flow around your system and boost you from the inside out. It's easy to brush this off, or forget to do it, or only do it from time to time, but if you make it a commitment and a constant practice it'll become a part of your life. Watch out for sabotaging yourself, because of your resistance to what being grateful will give you (happiness, a better life, more love, freedom and so forth). Learn to catch yourself out when you resist or sabotage.

Go crazy with your gratitude. First thing in the morning when you wake up, thank your bed for supporting you, thank your sleep for restoring you, thank your breakfast for nourishing you. Do it throughout the day: thank people for sending you great emails, new opportunities, new recommendations, their support, their compliments. Do it in bed at night; wrap up the day by listing the main things that happened that you are grateful for. Share the list with your partner, and do it together. Teach your kids and do it with them. Make it fun and something you love doing.

2. SHOWER YOURSELF WITH LIGHT. Sit somewhere quiet and close your eyes. Take some deep breaths into your body, breathe out with a big sigh and relax. Begin to visualise a big ball of shimmering white light above the top of your head. Take time to imagine the texture, shape and form. Is it moving? Is it hovering? Notice how big it is. Watch it open up into a big rainforest-style showerhead and turn on. See the powerful rain of white light showering down onto you and feel yourself getting drenched with white light. Stay with this for five minutes or more, all the while visualising this powerful shower of white light cascading down onto your body and into your cells. Breathe it in, and receive all this white light coming from the shower. Be grateful for the energy shower; thank the showerhead for opening, and then bring your awareness back into the present.

3. PUT YOUR POSITIVE PANTS ON. Words are energy, and using positive words in your vocabulary is like music to the soul. Using more positive words instantly raises your vibes and pings you up into glory state. Examples include: happiness, joy, expansion, rejoicing, celebration, harmony, nourishment, powerfulness, richness, abundance.
Experiment to find out which words make you feel high. Notice the words that resonate with you, and make a list. Stick it somewhere you'll notice it to remind you!

CHAPTER

Change the Rules

In this Tonic, you will learn:

♦ About the rules ♦
♦ Where the rules come from ♦
♦ How to make your own rules ♦

We've created a world around us full of rules. We have rules for every aspect of our lives. Most of the time we don't even realise the rules are there, yet we follow them and bow to them slavishly like the good humans that we are.

But following the rules holds us back. They limit our potential, our beliefs and our drive for bigger and better things. They keep us firmly in our comfort zone, safe and stuck. We do things we don't really want to do, and pursue careers we're told to because it's supposedly what's best for us.

The rules are structures in your mind. We're living from our mind, and allowing our thoughts to control our lives.

But your mind is not you; you are not your mind. Try

repeating this mantra out loud to separate yourself from your mind and your thoughts:

"I am not my mind. I am not my thoughts."

Repeat several times and see if you notice any difference.

The unwritten rules have the most power over us. Whenever anything is hidden away from our awareness, it wields extra power over us and has more control over our lives.

We have rules covering:

1. What we eat: no white bread or sugar because they're bad for us.
2. What we wear: not white jeans because they make us "look fat", or (for men) patterned shirts that make us "stand out".
3. Where we work: we accept sensible jobs with sensible perks because it makes Mum proud (even though it makes us unhappy).
4. When we work: between the hours of 9am and 6pm, because that's the rules, although we often stay later because it's the done thing (and makes us look good).
5. When we sleep: we're in bed by 11pm, and sleep for eight hours or we risk not being on form.
6. When we get married and have children: before the age of 30 or 35, depending on who you're listening to.

7. Who we date: they have to be good-looking and earn lots of money or we avoid them.

8. Social media: we have to post on Instagram/Facebook/Twitter at least three times a day to make sure people see us.

Not all of these rules will resonate with you, but you'll have your own variations in the big book of rules inside your mind. And when you don't follow them, you tell yourself off and believe you've failed, which doesn't feel very good at all. Especially because you keep telling yourself off every time you go rogue and break the rules, which (if you're anything like me) happens pretty often.

Set yourself free

When you were young, did you have to do things a certain way?

Most parents bring up their children to know the difference between right and wrong, and put certain rules into place to underline this. If you don't follow the rules, you get into trouble. A part of us still believes this will happen in adult life, so we still follow the rules put in place when we were young. This behaviour of rule-following is so ingrained from an early age that most of us are still afraid of getting into trouble, or being grounded, or sent upstairs to our room, or denied love, or whatever else happened to us when we disobeyed the rules. We might not be aware of it, but we still follow the rules without thinking.

When we go to school, we're taught a whole new set of rules.

And when we start a new job, more rules.

And when we enter into a new relationship, we each bring our own rulebooks and we fall out over our rules.

Let's be honest: there are certain rules we should follow, such as picking up your dog's poo, paying taxes, not driving on the pavement, sticking to 30-mile-an-hour speed limits where instructed. These are rules for good, so use your common sense around this.

But too many self-imposed rules can stop you from being your true self, and living in authenticity.

It's time to set yourself free of these rules, and make your own – or don't make any at all.

When you start your own business, you get to create what you want to create, and talk about what you do in your own way. You realise that there's no "right" way of doing things; there's your brilliant way, and that's the best way for you.

When you create your own rules, you only have yourself to answer to, and that's how it should be.

Don't let other people influence how you live your life. Follow your own way of doing things, follow your intuition and follow your heart.

Tools to help you make your own rules:

1. WHAT RULES DEFINE YOU? It's good to become aware of the rules that are governing your life. Make a list of all the ones you feel you have to adhere to. In which areas of your life are you strict on yourself? Be honest; no one will see the list but you. For example:

- I only allow myself 20 minutes to get lunch.
- I only eat dessert on my birthday.
- If I go out drinking, I work extra hard at the gym the next day.
- I leave work only once my boss has gone home.
- I don't ride my bike on main roads.
- I don't go to the doctor in working hours.

Recognising that you are following rules is half the battle. Watch out for them in everyday life and think about how they are holding you back.

2. EMBRACE THE NEW. If you're going to have rules, make them positive rules about caring for yourself. Positive rules can enhance your life and aid your development. For example:

- Every morning I meditate for 20 minutes.
- Every Tuesday I book a few hours off for "me" time.
- Every six months I do a three-day juice cleanse.
- Every week I make some time for my own creative activities.

—31—

Be a Spiritual Gangster

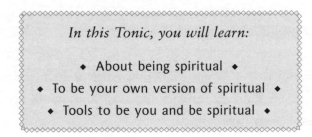

In this Tonic, you will learn:

◆ About being spiritual ◆
◆ To be your own version of spiritual ◆
◆ Tools to be you and be spiritual ◆

As I explained in Chapter 14, the word "spirituality" conjures up certain ideas, words or feelings depending on your beliefs, experiences and influences.

For me, being spiritual is essentially about believing that we're all connected through energy, spirit and the divine inner light which resides within us and everyone else on this planet. Spiritual people believe we are more than the physical body. We realise there's much more to life. We believe in energy being all around us, and within us. When I meet someone spiritual, I sense an inner calm about them, and an inner knowledge that everything is actually OK.

Being spiritual is about loving yourself and others, respecting nature, the planet and everyone who resides on it. When you're filled with spiritual energy, you feel more inspired to achieve your goals and live a greater life. Everybody can be divine, cosmic, transcendent, because by our very nature as human beings, we're all fuelled and supported by a great spiritual life-force from the source.

Let's work more on integrating spirituality into our systems. We would all like to have a more spiritual life, whether we're open to admitting it yet or not. It's our true nature, and we're already moving towards it.

Being cosmic

How does the word "spiritual" make you feel?

Do you shut down?

Does it make you want to run away?

Do you cringe when you hear it?

Or are you open to understanding more?

Your personal beliefs and associations with the word "spiritual" will be influenced by the opinions of your family and friends. You'll also be shaped by views from the media. Everyone has an opinion, mostly based on what they have read or inherited rather than what they've actually experienced for themselves.

It's important to be honest with yourself and admit how much resistance you have towards spirituality, love and light – you'll definitely have some. Everyone does, even the most spiritual of teachers. The journey is about recognising the resistance (it's great at disguising itself) and accessing it to bring more awareness to it, and finally to release it. In doing this, we allow more of our enlightened spiritual self to rise up.

How much of you is in the cosmic closet? Are you hiding away or in denial for some reason?

You don't need to know the reason why; it's enough to become aware that you're hiding. It's much easier to stay in the closet, as we care too much about what people think of us, but the rewards when you come out are amazing.

As soon as you have a spiritual experience, you become much more open to the whole concept of it. You've felt something, seen something or had a revelation about something. You've experienced it, so it's no longer purely abstract.

I've always believed in the power of experiencing something first and then defining what I've experienced. I've had many supernatural encounters, which I haven't been able to define in words alone. This often happens in spiritual workshops or training when I'm in full transformation mode and doing a lot of inner healing work. I'm repeatedly lost for words, but it doesn't matter because I don't feel the need to explain or try to rationalise what I've experienced.

More often than not we stay closed to new experiences, particularly the spiritual ones, because we can't find words to explain them. We miss out on incredible things because our mind doesn't allow us to participate in things we don't fully understand – which is a shame.

Life is for living and you don't want to miss out on anything, especially spirituality, which brings magic and excitement.

Let's together be open to the idea that:

---

*You can be spiritual on your terms, in your own
unique way, in your own time, in your own
clothes!*

Incorporating spirituality into your everyday life can be easy.

You don't need to make any huge changes, or leave your
job, or sell your clothes, or join a church or indeed a cult, or
do anything else you might think you'd have to do to become
more celestial.

Many celebrities are very open about having a spiritual
practice: these include: Arianna Huffington, Oprah Winfrey,
Ellie Goulding, Russell Brand, Gwyneth Paltrow, Richard
Gere, Angelina Jolie and Tina Turner.

It was a huge revelation when I realised "being spiritual"
could be on my terms. I breathed a big sigh of relief. I could
be spiritual and make it my own. I could be cosmic and cool.
I could be blissful and still buy the products I love. I could wear
sassy clothes, and do all the things I love doing. I didn't
have to sacrifice my material possessions and devote myself
entirely to serving others. I could spend money on things that
mattered to me, and travel to exotic places to recharge. In fact,
this is encouraged.

This is the age of the modern spiritualista, and making your
own rules is completely acceptable.

Be your version of spiritual

Be a spiritual gangster, or not if it's not your thing. Be an enlightened fashionista, teacher, nurse, designer, TV presenter, receptionist, lawyer. Blend it with whatever you want, be you and be glorious. Mix it with different schools of thought, modern spiritual beliefs, shamanism, religious beliefs, etc. These are your rules on your terms!

Modern spirituality to me means a delightful union between the material world and the cosmic world. Wherever they meet is the sweet spot; that's where you'll find your own version of spiritual. Everyone's spiritual self will be different and unique, because everyone in the world is different and unique.

In a few short years, being spiritually enlightened is likely to be the norm, so why not get a head start now?

What might your expression of your mystical self be?

How would you express your spiritual self?

◆ A cosmic crystal-lover?
◆ A healthy hipster?
◆ A flower-headband-wearing hippy?
◆ A raw food naturalista?
◆ A passionate leggings-wearing yoga girl?

How can you unleash this magnificent side of yourself onto the world? What do you want to attract into your new world?

You can be divine in your own way. Everyone is on their own unique path to spirituality.

Tools to be your version of spiritual:

1. CREATE YOUR SPIRITUAL LIFE. Take a big sheet of white paper and write a heading at the top: "My spiritual life". This exercise is about creating your own version of spiritual, so you can move out of your preconceived opinions and beliefs, and open your mind even more. The more open you are, the more you transform. Write down words to create a visual version of your new cosmic world and energy within in it. Run wild, have no limitations. There are no wrong words. Use pictures to help create a visual version; if you like you can put them on a Pinterest board.

My Words Are:

- Modern
- Yoga
- High vibes
- Divine
- Glorious
- Blissful
- Celestial
- Cool

- Cosmic love
- Sacred
- Space
- Galaxies
- Crystals
- Candles
- Unicorns
- Enchantment

2. FIND YOUR TRIBE. Notice which spiritual teachers or guides you resonate with, and follow them. Get inspired, go to their events and meet other people who go. You're sure to find things in common and you'll feel uplifted by each other because you're all there for a similar purpose. You can share stories and get tips from each other. It's a great way to find your "tribe".

3. GET CLEAR ON YOUR SPIRITUAL RESISTANCE. If you noticed resistance or objections coming up during this chapter, or your mind questioning anything, simply honour your resistance to spirit, to love, to expansion, and to being more connected to your spiritual self. Allow the fear to be there. It's normal and it's best to acknowledge its presence so you can address it and eventually clear it away.

CHAPTER

Be the Real You

In this Tonic, you will learn:

♦ About being real ♦

♦ How and why you're holding back ♦

♦ Tools to be more authentic ♦

Your true authentic self comes from inside of you. It's an energy or an essence which emerges straight from your inner source. You can't label it or bottle it or describe it in words, but you can feel it and you can be it. And that's the key here, to BE it.

Imagine your essence as an elixir, a magic, sparkling light emerging from the darkness that is coming to brighten up the world. It radiates naturally from within you, without you having to do anything. This happens more freely the clearer you are and the more of your baggage you have healed.

You can also intend to connect to your essence and radiate it out. The clearer you become, the more it will radiate.

Isn't it time you gave yourself the space and commitment to allow more of your authentic powers to emerge? Life

245

becomes so much easier when you do, because then you're not going against the grain. You are in the flow of life and aligned to your higher purpose.

Hiding the real you

Do you change or adapt depending on the people you're around?

Do you sometimes feel like a fake?

Or worry about being found out?

We're often hiding our full selves, toning ourselves down. We live in fear of what could happen if we emerged full power and showed all of ourselves. Deep down, we're petrified of being judged or criticised for our work or opinions, or rejected by our peers.

Perhaps we believe that the world isn't ready for our unique gifts. We have a million excuses not to show ourselves, meaning right now we're suppressing our abilities and talents, depriving the world of new and dazzling treasures.

How might you be holding back in your life? There's no need to overanalyse; go with whatever springs to mind.

◆ Are you sitting on the fence about changing career?

◆ Wanting to start a new venture but you don't believe it'll work?

◆ Yearning for your inner minx to come out in the bedroom but you're afraid of what you'll unleash?

◆ Desperate to say how much you love your partner, and how devastated you would be if anything should come between you, but too nervous to voice the words?

◆ Thinking of turning down that incredible job/gig/opportunity because of your anxiety?

I could continue, but you get the idea.

If you're unsure if this applies to you, be open-minded and keep reading. This speaks to most of us to some degree or another, and it's uncomfortable to face why you're holding back. Your ego doesn't want you to recognise this part of you. Your ego is worried about losing its job. It knows that once you unleash the real you, you'll be more authentic, happier, clearer and more committed to listening to and acting on your inner guidance. You'll then be less inclined to listen to the bossy ego who's been ruling your life thus far.

Working with my clients has helped me to realise how many of us are holding back – even the superstars. It's now more important than ever to realise "how" we're holding back, and do something about it. Deep down there's a desire to move into a more expansive area of life, to widen our experiences and receive more, leading to all kinds of possibilities.

Staying in the spiritual closet

We live in fear of what might happen. We stay in the closet for good reason, or so the ego believes.

At some point we will be gently coaxed out. If we don't listen it'll be more of a push, and if we still don't listen we'll get a shove, a kick or a slap in the face. This can provoke a crisis or an illness of some sort. In my case, I was chronically stressed before I reached the clear realisation that I couldn't go on living my life the way I was.

This is not an unknown force at work; it's your higher self who attracts in these big signs in the hope that you'll listen and wake up. If that's hard to believe, no worries; it'll make sense at some point, a little bit further on in your journey.

Some people won't like you, or won't want to hear what you have to say. You absolutely cannot please everybody, so stop trying. This is one of the hardest lessons to learn.

"You can be the ripest, juiciest peach in the world, and there's still going to be somebody who hates peaches."
– Roald Dahl

At times you will trigger people, anger them, upset them and they won't know why. Often it is because they are avoiding facing up to something from their past and you are a mirror reflecting their pain back at them. Learn to let it go. The right people will be around you at the right time. You cannot force anyone to like you. Maybe they will at some point, and perhaps they never will. Let it go. You are amazing and doing the absolute best you can and that is always enough. Their story is theirs and not yours to fix. Even if you understand more about them than they do about themselves, they have to reach their own conclusions. You can be there if and when they fall down, and offer comfort and reassurance to help them rebuild.

Don't let this be a reason to hold your own self back. Check in with you now. Can you relate to this? If you're completely honest with yourself, have you kept yourself back to fit in with others? Are you doing it now?

Reflect on what you've learned about yourself so far. Are you clearer on how you want to improve your life? Do you know what you want to do? What steps to take?

Whether you're clearer or not, the most important thing is to relax and know that things will fall into place. Use the Tools below to help you feel reassured and give you peace of mind.

Tools to be authentically you:

1. "I AM THAT I AM." This is a very powerful phrase. The energy of the words activates your inner essence, brightens your inner light and encourages your authentic self to step forwards. Say this out loud to yourself. Say it slowly and feel the energy of the words. Notice how your body responds on the inside of you. Can you feel a shift, either a soft, subtle shift or a strengthening? Try moving to various parts of your body and repeating the phrase. Move to your heart centre and say "I am that I am" into your heart. Can you feel your heart become stronger? Move to your hips and pelvis and repeat the phrase there. Can you feel your hips and pelvis become stronger? Explore and play around with this. Use it to feel your power in a stronger way, from the inside out.

2. I DESERVE IT ALL. We can get stuck in the belief that we don't deserve to have it "all", meaning the positivity and goodness we'll receive when we tap into our authentic centres and radiate out our inner light. Realising that we do, with absolute certainty, deserve it all – and more – means we'll be more easily able to connect to the real, authentic self and strengthen this part.

Say to yourself "I deserve it" and, at the same time, move your hand and arm in towards yourself, as if you're beckoning someone towards you. Use this gesture to bring it in. Repeat a few times, and make it part of your practice.

3. SELF-ACCEPTANCE. Learn to accept yourself. Stop judging yourself. Use the tapping tool. Bunch one of your hands into a fist and gently tap into the 'V' at the centre of the collarbone while repeating the following affirmations of acceptance out loud:

- I accept myself
- I believe in myself
- I honour myself

Make this part of your daily practice.

4. ASK A FRIEND. Get your BFFs to write down ten things they love about you, and send them to you in an email. Collect the love letters all together, and read them out loud to yourself. Notice how much love you have around you, and how much people love you for who you are. Your closest friends see the real you all the time, even when you're pretending! Reading these love letters will help you feel more confident in yourself, and supported no matter what you do.

Nourish Your Garden

In this Tonic, you will learn:

◆ Why self-care is so important ◆
◆ Tools to create your self-care practice ◆

Self-care is making the decision to prioritise yourself, invest in yourself and give yourself the care and attention you deserve. The act of self-care is vital when you're going through any kind of process or healing journey. The more open you become, the more important the need to practise self-care.

When we care for ourselves, we naturally feel more loved and cared for from the inside out. When we're feeling low, stressed, tired or sick with illness, all we really crave is to be loved and given love from ourselves. When we're taking time to nourish ourselves, we're really happy and we blossom.

Your natural state is like the Garden of Eden: lush, rich, abundant and vibrant. Imagine this is inside you, like a beautiful secret garden that you have to maintain and tend to. You pull out the weeds by the roots, trim the grass, prune the plants and sow seeds and shoots. You need to keep feeding and nourishing the garden to make sure everything on the inside is cared for, blooms and flourishes.

This is you. You need to be maintained. You need to water your plants.

All of us need a self-care routine. A practice that we commit to every day, morning or evening. It becomes a habit, and one you'll need to increase during stressful times in your life. When the busyness increases, so should your self-care. Balance out the stress, and invest in yourself with positive, nourishing things.

When going through particularly tough times – when you're feeling very down or low on energy, and nothing seems to be going right – take a full day to focus on caring for yourself. Book a massage, a pedicure, a new haircut. Apply a facemask, file your nails, try a delicious-smelling body oil. Eat gorgeous, healthy foods and drink loads of water. Take some gentle exercise and talk to your wisest, most nourishing friends.

It's all about loving yourself – the message that is at the heart of this book. Although this Tonic comes at the end, self-love, which is manifested in self-care, is fundamental to our wellbeing, energy and happiness. It's the starting point from which everything else flows gracefully.

Good luck as you create your own self-care practice and watch your life flourish.

Tools for practising self-care:

1. MORNING MEDITATION. A morning meditation practice is non-negotiable. It's the most aligned, in-tune and positive way to start your day. When you get into the habit of doing this, and have to miss it for some reason, even once, you realise how much of an effect meditation has on your life.

2. EPSOM BATHS. Bathing in salts has changed my life. Our bodies are naturally deficient of minerals and salts. When you bathe, minerals can be absorbed into your system easily through the skin. Bathing in salts is also very relaxing.

3. DUVET DAYS. Book yourself a day off to lie in your bed and snuggle up. It's nice to have a hot-water bottle to add to the warmth and cosiness. If you don't like to stay in bed, have a couch day with a blanket and plenty of cushions. Listen to your body and it'll tell you when you need a day like this. There are times when you simply need a day to rest and recharge.

4. LUNCHTIME BREAK. Break for lunch, go outside and breathe some fresh air; go for a walk. It's important to reset your energy, so move away from your laptop and take a break. You'll then have fresh energy to tackle whatever's left to do in the afternoon.

5. DRINK PURE WATER. Up to 60 per cent of the human body is made of water, so we need water to survive – but most of us don't drink enough of it. Water gives us life. It runs through our systems and maintains our natural flow. Water equals pureness and clarity for the mind and body. If we don't drink enough, we get headaches, tiredness, low energy and many other symptoms. Every morning as soon as you wake up, drink two glasses of water to hydrate your system and wash out the toxins created during your sleep.

6. MASSAGE, GROOMING AND FACIALS. Male or female, these should be part of your non-negotiable self-care routine. And if you're worried about the money, don't be. You'll find the money when you have the intention to look after yourself. Invest in yourself. It doesn't always have to cost money: take it in turns with your partner to treat each other at home. The important thing is making the time. Don't keep putting it off. You are more precious than that.

7. HUG SOME TREES. This is life-changing. Whenever I feel heavy in my shoulders, or as if I'm carrying heavy energy after an event, I will head to the park and hug a tree. The tree absorbs the negativity, and I feel it leaving my body. It's magic. Trees are magical healers, and they're free!

PART THREE

Moving Forwards

Final Word From Me

Freedom is what we long for.

Freedom from the past.
Freedom from old emotions.
Freedom from pain and heartbreak.
Freedom from illness and disease.
Freedom from negative thought patterns.
Freedom from control and anxiety.
Freedom from limiting beliefs.

Set yourself free. Set your soul free, and let your spirit soar.

Thank you, thank you, thank you for reading this book. I am honoured you stuck with it, and tried my LifeTonics. I hope they have served you in the perfect way, and I'm so excited you allowed me to support you on this magical healing journey.

Sending love and infinite light your way.

You are an incredible human being, and your commitment and dedication to reading this book and practising the Tools will help you shift your world.

Further Resources

The LifeTonic Audio Accompaniment
To enrich your healing experience, and further deepen your practice, go to my website to find audio resources to help you. You'll find meditations, wisdom and exercises to heal your modern woes by releasing your blocks, limitations and pains from the past.

LifeTonic TV
I have recently launched LifeTonic TV on YouTube. Watch my videos and join in with the LifeTonic community, I'll be sharing Tools, techniques and spiritual wisdom about improving relationships, finances, confidence, anxiety, stress and everything in between.

www.youtube.com/JodyShield

The LifeTonic Book Community
Come and be part of our Facebook LifeTonic community, and you will receive support, healing and nourishment every day.

Head to Facebook at /JodyShieldHealing for information about how to join or email hello@jodyshield.co.uk.

Events, one-on-one sessions and online courses

Join me in-person or online at the group healing events I hold around the world.

I offer private sessions in London or via Skype. These are healing sessions working on your issues, targeting the root cause and reasons why you're struggling. I work with your memories, emotions, spiritual aspect, physical aspect, mental aspect and your energy field, to receive relevant insight and information that helps you understand more, and to shift from the inside-out.

You can also purchase my online courses, download meditations, buy products that I use and get lots of inspiration from my website. You'll also find further information on all of the above at:

www.jodyshield.co.uk

Join me on social media

Twitter: @jodyshield
Facebook: @jodyshieldhealing
Instagram: @jodyshield

Inspiring books I've read during my journey

- Brown, Brené, *Daring Greatly: How the Courage to be Vulnerable Transforms the Way We Live, Love, Parent and Lead*, Avery, New York, 2015
- Cantwell, Marianne, *Be a Free Range Human*, New York, 2013
- Ford, Debbie, *The Dark Side of the Light Chasers*, London, 2001

- Gilbert, Elizabeth, *Big Magic: Creative Living Beyond Fear*, London, 2015
- Hunt, Anna, *The Shaman in Stilettos*, London, 2012
- Ortner, Nick, *The Tapping Solution*, London, 2013
- Shoshanna, Brenda, *Zen and the Art of Falling in Love*, New York, 2004
- Singer, Michael A., *The Untethered Soul: The Journey Beyond Yourself*, Oakland, California, 2007
- Weiss, Brian L., *Many Lives, Many Masters*, London, 1994

Recommended playlist

I highly recommend that you buy the music and support these artists:

Deuter, "Temple of Silence" (*Garden of the Gods*), 2001
Deuter, "Hollow Bamboo 1" (*Flowers of Silence*), 2014
Bliss, "Shiv Shakti" (*A Hundred Thousand Angels*), 2004
Bliss, "This Love" (*A Hundred Thousand Angels*), 2004
Bliss, "Sunrise" (*A Hundred Thousand Angels*), 2004
Ashana, "Still Light on Water" (*Jewels of Silence*), 2008
Ashana, "Soulmerge" (*Jewels of Silence*), 2008
Ashana, "Vision" (*Jewels of Silence*), 2008
Sinead O'Connor, "The Healing Room" (*Faith and Courage*), 2000
Mirabai Ceiba, "Ong Namo" (*Awakened Earth*), 2011

My favourite motivational speakers and teachers

- Damien Wynne, founder of Light Grids http://damien-wynne.de/en/

- Marianne Williamson http://marianne.com
- Marie Forleo http://www.marieforleo.com
- Gabby Bernstein http://gabbybernstein.com
- Tony Robbins http://www.tonyrobbins.com

Useful organisations

- www.drinkaware.co.uk/alcohol-support-services gives a list of different organisations who can help with alcohol addiction.
- www.talktofrank.com is a valuable resource for people who think they have a problem with drugs, and for those who are worried about friends' or family members' drug habits.
- www.abuse-survivors.org.uk gives information and support for anyone affected by abuse.
- www.anorexiabulimiacare.org.uk is a good first stop for anyone with an eating disorder.
- www.samaritans.org is a wonderful telephone helpline for anyone who is feeling desperate or struggling with life.

Acknowledgements

I'm deeply grateful to all of my "teachers" in life for everything you've taught me. Especially the following people for your encouragement, your wisdom, your inspiration, your beautiful presence and for cheering me on at every hurdle:

Damien Wynne for your pioneering teachings, your deep belief in my talents, gifts and your endless support. The amazing team at Lululemon UK and Lululemon Global Vancouver for all your constant love and encouragement, and for pushing me further into my power! To Ged Ferguson, Bengt Thomson, Rebecca Campbell, Alan Dolan and anyone else who has supported my healing during the writing of this book. To Gillian Campbell and family for your blessings. To Valeria my literary agent, and the lovely team at Yellow Kite, including: Liz, Emma, Auriol, Lauren, Catriona. To my beautiful soul sisters: Lauren, Dalia, Carly, Tanya, Becky, Charlie, Melissa, Gill, Cher, Persia, Selina, Ashley – you've all inspired me to keep going during the tough times.

To Freya, Saphia, Claire and Olly for coming along for the journey and your amazing support.

To all my clients and group clients over the past few years who've been to all the events, talks and sessions.

My supportive and loving family who always believed in me and my vision: Juliet (my mentor), John (my biggest fan), Cosmo, Nicki and my loving Nana Doris and Anne Wolff (I know you'd be proud).

Finally, my rock (and fiancé), Paul. We met at Burning Man all those years ago, and despite all the transformation I've been through, you haven't left my side since.